The Cambridge Manuals of Science and
Literature

THE ROYAL NAVY

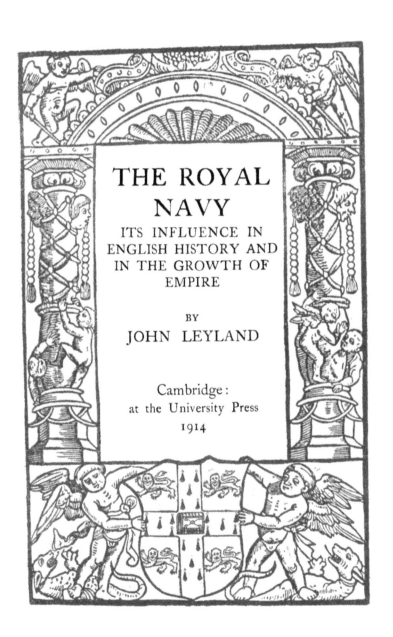

THE ROYAL NAVY

ITS INFLUENCE IN ENGLISH HISTORY AND IN THE GROWTH OF EMPIRE

BY

JOHN LEYLAND

Cambridge:
at the University Press
1914

CAMBRIDGE UNIVERSITY PRESS
Cambridge, New York, Melbourne, Madrid, Cape Town,
Singapore, São Paulo, Delhi, Tokyo, Mexico City

Cambridge University Press
The Edinburgh Building, Cambridge CB2 8RU, UK

Published in the United States of America by Cambridge University Press, New York

www.cambridge.org
Information on this title: www.cambridge.org/9781107632714

© Cambridge University Press 1914

First published 1914
First paperback edition 2011

A catalogue record for this publication is available from the British Library

ISBN 978-1-107-632714 Paperback

*With the exception of the coat of arms at
the foot, the design on the title page is a
reproduction of one used by the earliest known
Cambridge printer, John Siberch, 1521*

PREFACE

ONE object of this little Manual is to bring within the compass of a few brief chapters a general view of the nature, character and development of the British Navy. A larger purpose is to shew the influence of the Navy in safeguarding the independence and security of the country, and the part it has played in promoting the growth and upholding the integrity of the Empire.

The influence of the sea pervades our history, and has been instrumental in the shaping of our national institutions and character. It is therefore preeminently worthy of study. By our maritime supremacy and our wardship of the seas the Empire has come into being, and without that wardship the Empire would have ceased to be.

Notwithstanding all that has been written during recent years concerning the Navy, there is still a want of understanding amongst the people at large of these matters of fundamental importance. When questions arise in relation to Imperial Defence, opinions are formed which are based on imperfect knowledge of the principles which underlie our maritime history. Even subjects which touch our island defence are handled with little reference to the lessons of the past, which are the surest guide to the policy of the future. We may read, in this history, of safety won by the exercise of wise foresight in maintaining the essentials for naval sufficiency, and of advantages lost and interests imperilled by the want of such foresight.

An outstanding and characteristic feature of naval administration in the past has been its exhibition of a strange ebb and flow in the provision of the prime essentials for naval security, periods of development and efficiency having been succeeded by periods of decline and decay, in which sometimes Fortune has favoured us by blinding or weakening our adversaries, when our own preparations might not have availed. That we must not, through neglect, entrust our welfare to the favour of Fortune is a lesson which shines forth plainly from all our history.

We learn, too, from naval history that we possess advantages, by virtue of our island position and the communications of the Empire being by sea, that are not possessed by nations which are parts of the continent, and are therefore influenced by the imperious demands of land power. We infer that there is something really different in our national character from that of continental nations, and that this difference, combined with the advantages of our geographical situation, has fitted us for success at sea in a manner which has been denied to other races. History warns us that we must guard ourselves from throwing away or diminishing the advantage which we enjoy in the fact that our security and our influence are based upon power of command at sea.

The lessons of this book are not insistently put forward. Rather, it is left to the reader, with some indications, to deduce the meaning of history from its events and circumstances. The index will shew where questions relative to invasion, blockade and other conditions are illustrated. In the same way he may discover the evils that have arisen, and may arise, from naval and military misunderstandings, and from disputations within the service itself. The book shews how the Navy has on several occasions been the essential factor in the success of military operations, in circumstances hardly alluded to in our history books.

To bring before the reader these and other essential things is the object of the Manual, but, in suggesting the lessons of a philosophic study of naval history, the instrument whereby maritime influence has been exercised, and the incidents of its exercise, occupy a large part of the book. The Navy itself and its achievements are, indeed, in the foreground, with something of the picturesqueness of naval character, and, though the compass of the book is but small, few aspects of naval history have been altogether neglected. The ships of successive periods, the personnel and the conditions of naval life, the great personalities of naval history, administration, strategy, tactics, and the battles and events, with brief indications of salient features—all these have their place in the book.

The author expresses his indebtedness to many volumes in the wide literature of naval and other history. He gives in a short bibliography some indication of the best books relating to successive periods and subjects. It is gratifying that in the series of manuals in which this book appears, is a volume by Mr J. R. Thursfield dealing in a masterly manner with some special branches of naval strategy. Finally the author desires to place on record his especial obligations, for counsel and assistance in relation to this book, to his old friend and colleague Commander C. N. Robinson, R.N.

JOHN LEYLAND.

St George's Day, 1914.

CONTENTS

CHAPTER I

BEFORE we have advanced very far in this book we shall discover that the influence of the sea permeates our history deeply, and has in a large measure determined our national development and character. Whatever might be the importance relatively to other countries of a small island kingdom lying off the coast-line of the continent of Europe, its history must be most worthy of study, because essentially different from that of any part of that continent. The sea, which has always been a barrier, passed with greater or less difficulty, has for centuries also been a pathway, and in these two features of sea influence—the barrier and the pathway—lie the conditions which have shaped and dominated our English nation, and have given us our imperial heritage.

The sea has never, in its own nature, been an impassable barrier. Hardy seamen in all ages have traversed it. It has required organized forces for its proper control and mastery, and, in early times, when such forces did not exist, or existed only intermittently, it was crossed according to the measure of the skill, hardihood and good fortune of the seamen who navigated it. When fleets came into being, formed of ships of war, or ships capable of fighting, as forces tending towards permanency, the barrier grew more secure, and seafaring qualities alone did not suffice for the passage. There were required fighting capacity and sufficient material strength as well.

So secure did the barrier of the English seas become, owing to the inherent difficulties of sea transport, and the existence of sea forces to be overcome, that never since the Norman Conquest has it been passed by any body of enemies deserving to be taken into account. Out of these conditions have come some of our institutions and our conception of the principles and means of defence. There arose the view that our frontier should be the enemy's coast-line, which Raleigh, Howard and Drake expressed when they said that the enemy must be defeated on his own coasts, or before he could reach the English shore. Blake's view, that the object of the fleet was to " keep foreigners from fooling us," sprang from the same spirit and idea.

We shall deal very briefly with some parts of

our earlier history, partly because the evidences
are few, but mainly because later times will claim
greater attention. Our Saxon ancestors were seamen before they were Englishmen. Issuing in
their " keels " from the countries about the mouths
of the Elbe and the Weser, they were sea-wolves,
who captured what they could afloat, and carried
fire and sword into the countries they invaded and
afterwards occupied. The vessels in which they
came appear to have been from 70 to 100 feet
long, and from 16 to 18 feet wide, without decks,
and having a single mast and yard, with a large
square sail. Oars were used, and there was a
rudder or steering-oar over the right, or steer-
board side, or, as we now call it, the starboard,
much like a large paddle. Eventually England
was peopled by the new-comers, and how they
fought amongst themselves, how Augustine and
Christianity came, and how a single kingdom was
made out of many is in all our histories.

Offa is believed to have been the first English
ruler to build a considerable fleet, and it is said of
him that he left to his successors the maxim that
he who would be secure on land must be supreme
at sea. The danger came from Danes and Nor-
wegians, sea-rovers also, seeking better land than
their own, and plunder and outrage went where-
ever they sailed or strode.

Alfred, the greatest of all our early kings, knew that the sea could only be won by seafaring. He sent Othere to examine the northern coasts of Europe, who went as far as the White Sea, and Wulfstan to explore the Baltic, and in storm and tempest these early navigators and their comrades learned or manifested the art and craft of the sea. Alfred fought with the Danes in many a battle, and, for the work of the sea, the very navy for his purpose was to create. His " long ships " were an advance upon anything seen before, and some of them had more than sixty oars. They were better " sea boats," as we should say nowadays, than the earlier boats, as were the other types of vessels which Alfred also built. He was never content that they should be anything but better than the ships of his enemies, and, with that object, paid attention to the work at the ports, the selection of the wood, and the training and feeding of the men, thus creating a fleet that was capable of keeping the sea from summer until autumn.

Alfred's immediate successors did not let the naval forces decay, and Edgar greatly increased them, so that his fleets cruising round the coasts kept the sea clear of pirates, and it is related that eight vassal kings rowed his boat on the Dee. But when Edgar was dead, the wisdom of Offa and Alfred was forgotten, and the name of Ethelred

the Unready became a by-word. The Englishmen quarrelled amongst themselves, the pirate
scourge was renewed, and ultimately England lay at
the feet of the seafaring Danes and Scandinavians—
the Vik-ings, who, from every vic or wick in their
coasts, issued in war navies to seek the conquest
and spoil of England.

The northern ships were decked, and each bore
the emblem of her commander. They were carved
and adorned, and a device was at the prow, while,
carried externally round the bulwarks, were the
shields of the crew painted in many colours.
Canute's ship, the *Great Dragon*, was shaped rather
like a sea-monster, and was about 200 feet long,
and is said to have carried 70 oarsmen, besides
a crowd of fighting men. A Vik-ing ship discovered
at Gokstad in southern Norway measured 78 feet
in length, with 16 feet 6 in. beam. She had oak
planking, and the prow, gunwale, and sternpost
were carved. There were 32 oars, and the ship
carried at least three small boats. The method
of fighting was for a vessel to endeavour to sink
her enemy by ramming, or to run alongside, and the
matter was settled by boarding with battle-axes and
swords. The navy in those times was never a fixed
organization. There was no real distinction between a fighting and a trading ship. The King's
ships were manned by forces maintained under

the name of buscarles, and some of the great nobles had fleets which were at the disposal of the Crown.

Canute, the Dane, gave peace to his English people. Strong at sea beyond all his rivals, and having with him the ships of English thanes, his wars were abroad in the north, while prosperity grew in England. The pirates were quelled, and across the guarded pathway of the sea traders from Denmark and Scandinavia brought iron, skins, and ropes and masts for ships to our ports, and from other countries came silks, gold, silver, gems, wine, oil, ivory, brass, copper, and many other wares of use or necessity.

CHAPTER II

THE CONQUEROR'S SEA POWER

WE will pause to glance at one of the great turning points in English history. Harold had become king and had sworn an oath to William of Normandy, or was said to have sworn it, whereby William claimed the crown. Why did William become the Conqueror, and why was Harold overthrown?

Harold, like his father Godwin, was a man of ability, resource, activity and courage. As a

soldier he displayed great qualities. He was both
an organiser and a fighter. Experience of the past
had shown him that a fleet must be his only means
of keeping his enemy without, and he had a fleet
which is said to have been the largest ever seen on the
English coasts. He had an equal match in William,
who knew also that for his purpose a fleet was the
one thing without which nothing else could avail.
The Normans were the descendants of Scandinavian
settlers who, in William's time, had become more
French than Scandinavian, but the piratical blood
was in them, and they were as hard fighters
as could be found anywhere. William was the
strongest and most indomitable of them all. His
desperate courage, his fiery spirit, and the pitiless
tempest of his wrath made him a redoubtable
soldier and a foe to be feared. He shrank neither
from toil nor hardship. The soldier marched and
the pirate sailed in his blood. "So stark and fierce
was he," we read in the English Chronicle, "that
none durst resist his will."

But William had other qualities. Deep thought
was behind his sword. No sooner had his enterprise taken root in his mind than he began to lay
his plans and build his fleet. He bound his barons
and knights to him by promise of spoil. It was a
piratical undertaking he had in hand, but piracy
was a part of warfare. Bishops, priests, barons,

burghers and others came forward to offer ships
which they owned or would build. Trees were
cut down, and men were busy in the ports shaping
planks, framing ships and raising masts. Norman
ladies worked at standards and adornments. In
William's own ship, the *Mora*, Matilda, the Duke's
wife, placed a golden figure of a boy blowing a horn,
with his finger " pointing towards England," and
in the Bayeux tapestry that figure may be seen,
though, instead of the pointing finger, there is a
flag in the boy's hand. That famous tapestry is
not wholly accurate, but it shows us that each
ship had a single mast and a yard to carry the sail,
while the steersman sat at the stern, with his steering-oar working over the side. As to the number
of vessels employed, it is variously computed at
from about 700 to 1500. No one knows how many
men came with William. Some say 60,000. Probably 20,000, with horses and stores, would be nearer
the mark.

Harold and William were not the only figures
in the struggle. Harald Hardrada of Norway had
an ambition for conquest also, and Tostig, Harold's
jealous and disappointed brother, was confederated
with him. If Hardrada and Tostig were not the
puppets who danced to William's piping, it is clear
that William knew what Hardrada and the Earl
were about, and that they well served his turn.

How could he hope to bring his vast, unwieldy, overcrowded fleet across in the presence of the large fleet which Harold had at his command? As we have seen, in those times fleets could only be kept at sea or ready for sea in the summer, and that was no easy task. There existed no real permanent force, most of the seamen being fishermen or men engaged in the merchant trade of the sea, who had their own affairs to look after. Others seem to have been farmers, who had their crops to garner.

William took advantage of this circumstance. He appears to have encouraged Tostig to raid the Isle of Wight and the south and east coasts of England in the spring or early summer of 1066. Tostig was then driven off the mouth of the Humber by the northern Earls, and, in the meantime, Harold's fleet was hastily got ready for sea, and was cruising from May onward. William gathered his forces by the middle of August in the River Dives, where the chroniclers say he waited for what sailors call a "slant of wind," to carry him across. But he appears in reality to have been in no hurry. He knew both when to wait and when to strike. About the middle of September he moved up the coast to St-Valery-sur-Somme, and did not get a fair wind until the evening of September 27th.

What had happened meantime on the English

side ?   Tostig had fled with twelve ships from the Humber, and joined Hardrada, who was at the Orkneys with a large force.   They came south, landed their men, defeated those who opposed them, and seized York.   Hearing this disastrous news, Harold marched north, and, in a hard-fought battle, on September 25th—two days before William got his slant of wind—utterly defeated the northern invaders at Stamford Bridge, where both Hardrada and Tostig were slain.   While this was going forward Harold's fleet on the south-east coast, somewhere between the 8th and 12th September, had broken up and dispersed, the only barrier between William and the English shore being thus removed.

What was the cause of this failure ?   We are left in part to conjecture.   It is said that the sea-men could be held together no longer.   They were husbandmen, and had their harvests to gather. They had been tossed about since the early summer, which was a long time for the fleets of those days, while William's men had been assembled only for about six weeks.   This was due to the raiding of Tostig.   Harold's personal influence was no longer with his fleet.   Tostig and Hardrada had drawn him away.   The upshot was that the fleet dispersed, and that England was lost and won.

What a spectacle it must have been, looking

from Hastings Castle Hill, or the height of Beachy Head, when the Norman Duke's vast fleet anchored in Pevensey Bay! Hundreds of vessels were crowded along the vast curve of the shore. They drew little water, and as the keels grounded on the beach, the flapping sails came down, and the shouting men jumped overboard and waded up to the dry land. The horses were walked ashore, and the arms and some food-stores were soon on the beach.

It was not long afterwards that Taillefer on Senlac Hill threw up his sword and caught it, and threw it and caught it again, as he sang the song of Roland, and that the sanguinary struggle was fought in which Harold fell. But if his fleet had not broken up, the history of England would have been written differently. The potent influence of the sea had shaped anew the destiny of the land.

CHAPTER III

HOW MEDIÆVAL BATTLES WERE FOUGHT

THE Norman expedition of 1066 and the failure of Harold show clearly that in those times the sea was not a region that could be continuously or permanently controlled. Raiding could take place, and for centuries did take place, from one side of the Channel or the other, as the wind blew from the eastward or the westward. It was a barrier to one and a pathway to the other. The wind that enabled the Englishman to leave his ports kept the Frenchman at home, and when the wind shifted to the opposite quarter, the Frenchman could put to sea for an enterprise while the Englishman could with difficulty get his ships out of harbour. The blockade of ports was impossible, and the problem was to maintain fleets which might possess something of the character of permanency in their chief duty of being available at call as a Channel guard.

The warship was a merchant vessel equipped for fighting, and therefore by organizing the resources of the ports, it was possible to raise fleets with economy, while obtaining for the King's service the most experienced of seafaring men. In practice this was done mainly by employing the masters and men of the Cinque Ports. Shipping was taken up at other places, but in early times there was little of organization outside the fleets of the five merchant and fishing towns of Hastings, Sandwich, Dover, Romney and Hythe, to which Rye and Winchelsea were afterwards added. These ports possessed many men of hardy character skilled in handling the long ships, "busses," "cogs" and other vessels of those and later centuries. Various privileges were conferred upon the Barons of the ports in return for the services they rendered to the Crown, and their ships became a kind of Royal Navy, each of the ports being bound to provide a given number of ships for fixed periods.

The ships were bluff-bowed and capacious, but unhandy, and unable to advance except with the wind astern or in some quarter abaft the beam. They were decked and carried a single mast, with a large square sail. The bowsprit appeared in the 13th century, being in reality a foremast stepped well over the bow. The bow and stern curved upward, and when fitted for fighting, carried structures called castles—whence our modern fore-castle—from which points of vantage, as well as from nests or tops fixed on the masts, the fighting men could discharge arrows or other missiles. The navigator kept his course by the aid of the leads-man or the loom of the land, and at night the Pole-star was his mark and guide. In the Mediterranean other classes of ships were developed, including chiefly the swift galley, propelled by sail and the power of many oars, and there, too, originated the terrible Greek fire, being some kind of inflammable oil discharged on the ships of an enemy. This kind of attack seems rarely to have been used in the north. Ships of greater size were built as time went on, but all the early vessels were bigger than representations in manuscripts might lead us to suppose. The *Blanche Nef*, or White Ship, in the wreck of which, in 1120, Prince William and the flower of the English nobility were lost, is recorded to have pulled 50 oars, and to have had on board some 300 persons all told. But there were much bigger ships, and it is said that some pilgrim ships in the Mediterranean could carry 800 persons. This building of larger ships was coincident with the gradual silting up of the Cinque Ports, whereby Portsmouth, which had long been a port of assembly, came into greater prominence, and Dartmouth and Bristol were places of growing importance from which ships came for the service of the King.

Richard Cœur de Lion was the first English ruler to employ a fleet in a distant enterprise. This was in the Crusade of 1190, and it was no easy task to bring the huge flotilla through storm and tempest from Dartmouth and some French ports to Messina, where Richard joined the fleet, and then to Acre, and the success of the operation was an indication of the hardihood and seamanlike skill of the mariners. It was off Acre that Richard, in his long ship the *Trenchemer*, or as we should call her, Shearwater, had a terrible encounter with a big Saracen dromon. One chronicler calls her a great " busse," and another says that only Noah's Ark was bigger, for she carried 700 or 800 men under seven emirs. Showers of arrows and stones, sheets

of Greek fire, boarding and being driven back,
terrible hand-to-hand fighting, the fouling of the
dromon's rudder, and then the ramming of the
monster with the beaks of the galleys, whereby she
sank, were the features of the struggle. This was
a great victory of fighting seamanhood, for if the
Saracens had sunk the *Trenchemer*, the Crusaders
might never have taken Acre. It was in Richard's
time that the terribly severe code of naval discipline,
known as the Laws of Oleron, was introduced.

We can do little more than glance at four important naval actions fought nearer home in the 13th
and 14th centuries, which are typical of the work
of the fleet in those times and show its influence upon
national security. The first of these was the destruction of the French and Flemish fleet at Damme
in 1213. This was in the reign of John, who had
made some approach towards a naval establishment
and had appointed a " keeper of the Kings' ships."
Philip of France and the Count of Flanders had
assembled their fleet with the object of invading
England for the King's overthrow, but John's half-
brother, William Longsword, Earl of Salisbury,
took a fleet over to Damme, and after much hard
fighting, the ships there were destroyed. Here it
may be remarked that the action of Longsword in
destroying the enemy's ships before they could leave
port was precisely that advocated and practised

by Drake, more than three centuries later. By his
action the intended invasion came to nought.

Again, when the Barons were in revolt in 1217, a
seaman called Eustace the Monk, who had once been
in John's service, was aiding the French, and was
despatched with a convoy to help the English nobles.
His ships had been assembled at Calais and, with a
fair wind from the southward, he ran over towards
the English coast, with the intention of rounding
the North Foreland, and getting into the Thames.
Hubert de Burgh, King's Justiciary and Governor
of Dover Castle, prepared to intercept him, and,
saying " If these men once land England will be
lost," put to sea from Dover with the Cinque Ports
ships. He made as if he would fall upon Calais,
but his evident object was to get clear of the land,
and gain what old seamen called the "weather gage,"
that is to bring the wind behind him, so that he
might be able to bear down upon his enemy. Having
held his way long enough, he altered course, and fell
upon the Frenchmen's rear. It was fine seamanship, in the first English sea action of which there
is sure record, and Hawke, Rodney, Howe or
Nelson could hardly have done better. Clouds of
arrows covered the French ships, and unslaked
lime was thrown into the air to the blinding of many.
Some ships were sunk and others carried by boarding
with sword and axe and taken into Dover. Once

more the enemy had been destroyed before he could touch the land. Eustace paid the price, and his head was carried on a pole.

Now we pass on to the days of Edward III, whose gold noble shows the armed strength of England based on the sea, and who further organized the naval service and regulated the system of impressing men for the fleet. There had previously been great neglect, and the French had wrought havoc at Sandwich, Winchelsea, Rye, Hastings, Southampton and Portsmouth. They had even captured the King's own ship, the great "cog" *Christopher*. Their fleet was assembled at Sluys in 1340, and Edward, with about 250 sail, stood over to the Flemish coast, and the fleets met in mortal conflict, in the estuary on Midsummer day. In the English leading ships were posted archers, and in the French van were the *Christopher* and three other cogs captured from the English, all filled with Genoese cross-bowmen. Again there was great slaughter, for sea fighting in those days was peculiarly ferocious and sanguinary. Ship after ship was carried, until the enemy were almost completely destroyed, and quarter was neither asked nor given. This great victory gave Edward command of the sea for many a day, and France was afterwards invaded and the victory of Crecy won.

There was yet a sea action to fight, this time

with the Spaniards, for the King of Castile had gone
to the aid of the French with ships from Genoa, and
Basque seamen had ravaged the coasts. Then, in
1350, Carlos de la Cerda appeared with a fleet in
the Channel, and that battle was fought which was
known as " Les Espagnols sur Mer." Froissart has
filled a glowing page with the story, and tells of the
gallant bearing of the Black Prince and the flower
of English nobility, and of how the minstrels played
and Sir John Chandos sang to divert the mariners.
When the fleets met, there was sanguinary work
all along the line, and seventeen Spaniards were
taken, and the victory gave to England again the
security of the sea.

CHAPTER IV

SHIPS AND MEN

Now in a rapid course we will bridge a few
centuries, and see what things of interest we may
discover in our passage. The battle of Sluys and
that with the Spaniards marked the very height
of our sea power in mediæval times. There was
neglect afterwards, in consequence of which the
French landed in the Isle of Wight, and Folkestone,
Rye, Hastings, Winchester and other places were

again sacked or burnt. English seamen were as
brave as ever, but they could not serve the country
well without the support of Kings and Parliaments.
Chaucer has given us the type of them. The Earl
of Pembroke was soundly beaten by the Spaniards
under Ambrosio Bocanegra at Rochelle in 1372.
Pirates roved the seas, and a Scotsman named
Mercer was defeated, not by the King's forces,
but by those of John Philpot, a London merchant.
Henry V paid more attention to his fleet, and was
able to invade France and achieve the great victory
of Agincourt in 1415. In the next year the Duke
of Bedford inflicted a severe disaster on the French
at Harfleur, after a desperate action much like those
I have described. It was not, however, until the
times of Henry VII and his successor that there
was any real revival of English sea power. The
ships used by Hubert de Burgh had differed little
from those in which Canute and Tostig had
sailed the seas. When Edward III was besieging
Calais in 1347, he had a fleet drawn from most of
the ports in the Kingdom, some also from Ireland,
Flanders and even from Spain and Bayonne, consisting of 745 ships, and nearly 16,000 mariners,
besides fighting men. This will give an idea of the
enormous resources the country had even in those
days. Yarmouth, Fowey in Cornwall and Dartmouth
each sent more ships than London. Dependence

upon the Cinque Ports had begun to pass away, and the King's ships became more numerous. Guns appear to have been first mounted, or at least used, in ships by the Spaniards, in the battle of 1372 when the Earl of Pembroke was defeated. At first they were fired over the "gunwale," and the cutting of port holes came much later. The early guns were of indifferent value, firing stone shot, and they were made of hooped iron bars. It was a long time before they altogether displaced "springalds," "mangonels" and other machines for hurling masses of stone. Bows and arrows were included amongst the stores of ships as late as the reign of Elizabeth.

Some of the ships were brilliantly painted, and had great square sails showing the royal arms or the badges and devices of the nobles who sailed in them. Generally in later times there were three masts. The foremast leaned or "raked," as seamen say, forward and was practically a bowsprit, while the main mast carried a big square sail on a yard to which it was furled, and the mizzen or after mast was lateen rigged. National flags flew from the mast heads, with long streamers and pennants, and one red streamer was the sign of war and promised mercy to none.

In the time of Henry V the "great ship" had dethroned the cog from its position, but there

were still cogs, as well as carracks, barges and balin-
gers. The *Jesus* has been described as a ship of
1000 tons, the *Holy Ghost* of 760 tons, and the
Trinity Royal of 540 tons. In all Henry had a
fleet of 1400 vessels in 1415, raised from every port
in the Kingdom, ranging down from the "great
ship" to vessels of 20 tons.

By the time of Henry VII ships were much
better built, but some of them looked more formidable than they actually were. One big ship, the
Regent, launched in Reding Creek on the Rother in
1489 or 1490, had four masts and a bowsprit, and
carried 225 small guns called serpentines. She was
burnt in action off Brest with a French carrack, the
Marie la Cordelière, in 1512. Another ship built by
the seventh Henry, was the *Sovereign*, whose name
descended to the *Royal Sovereign* of modern days.
She was partly built under direction of Sir Reginald
Bray, architect of St George's Chapel, Windsor,
and [Henry VII's Chapel, Westminster, probably
from the remains of an older vessel, the *Grace à
Dieu*.

The most famous ship of Henry VIII was the
Henry Grace à Dieu, which was built or rebuilt at
Erith in 1514. She was probably begun as a reply
to the *Great Michael* of the Scottish King, which was
built about 1506, and is described by Pitscottie as
having been 240 feet long over all and 36 feet broad

within board, and as having "walls ten foot thick in the wall and boards." The *Henry Grace à Dieu* was a splendid vessel of imposing aspect, with two lines of guns on her lower decks, and a third line on her half deck and forecastle. Massive structures rose high at the bow and the stern, and at the latter position she had actually five tiers of guns and eight decks. Henry had also galleasses, and many vessels of other ratings, some of them with three or four masts and a bowsprit, mounting ten or a dozen guns on the broadside. The guns of the time were perhaps not far inferior to those which Nelson used.

In the days when ships were hired for war purposes, the men came with them, and the "master," who was a seaman to the core, sailed the ship, while the actual commander was the military officer who embarked with men at arms and archers. Admirals were appointed in Edward I's reign, and the development of the ranks of officers was progressive through the centuries. As to the seamen, when they were scarce they were seized and pressed into the service. There was a good deal of adventure in the sea career, and the promise of much spoil, but it was a hard life, with heavy punishments for small faults, some of them most barbarous and cruel. We should learn to love these men, for they suffered in cold and hunger, with food of the vilest, ever fighting with enemies, winds and waves, punished with brutality, and rewarded with little more than what they could hope to win in the harvest of capture at sea.

While ships were being built and manned by the Tudors, administrative organization was progressing. The dockyards at Portsmouth, Woolwich and Deptford were considerably increased, and under Henry VIII the Trinity House was established to regulate buoys, beacons and lighthouses. A proud consciousness of power was in the fleet. Ever since the days of Edward III and earlier we had claimed the sovereignty of the narrow seas—a political rather than a purely naval dominion. We had indeed claimed the salute as early as an ordinance of John in 1201. The thought that the sea must be " kept " is interwoven with our history. Originating in the need of suppressing piracy, through the agency of the mercantile ports, it assumed a larger meaning, and gave us the watchword of our policy. Power was inevitably bound up with jurisdiction, and even when Philip came to woo Queen Mary, Howard exacted the homage of the lowering of the Spanish topsails, before he saluted the Spanish King.

CHAPTER V

THE AGE OF DISCOVERY AND THE OVERTHROW
OF SPAIN

WE have traced the origin of the Navy in the centuries we have traversed, but if we would seek its beginning, as we know it to-day, in the character of an imperial Navy, we shall find it in the discoveries of the old navigators, and the enterprises of the merchants who followed them. In the ages we have so far surveyed the sea was a region from whose perils the mariners shrank, keeping within sight of the coasts, if only, like Shakespear's boatswain, they might have " room enough," and dreading the portents of the storms. But in the new age of discovery and of scientific navigation the sea became a pathway, and a means for the meetings and the rivalries of men. Its great figures, as Professor Seeley said, were not the Hotspurs of mediæval chivalry, nor the archers by whom Crecy was won, but " the hero buccaneers, the Drakes and Hawkinses, whose lives had been spent in tossing upon that ocean which to their fathers had been an unexplored unprofitable desert."

They were not Englishmen who led the van in the opening up of the world. We take proper pride in Sir Hugh Willoughby, who perished on the coast of Lapland, Chancellor who followed him, Borough who sailed between Novaya Zemlya and the mainland, and Pett who penetrated the Kara Sea, and we glory in the discoveries of Frobisher, Davis, Hudson and many more whose names are written on the maps of the great North-West. All were seeking the riches and splendours of the Oriental world. But they were the valiant captains of Prince Henry of Portugal, the Navigator, who pushed in successive voyages along the coasts of Africa until Bartholomew Diaz doubled the Cape of Storms, and Vasco da Gama was the first of modern men to reach India by sea. It was Amerigo Vespucci who gave his name to the American continent, which Columbus and his comrades and successors opened to the world—

"Who pushed his prows into the setting sun,
And made West East, and sail'd the Dragon's Mouth,
And came upon the Mountain of the World,
And saw the rivers roll from Paradise!"

It was Vasco Nuñez de Balboa who first set eyes upon the Pacific ; it was Magellan who clove his way through the straits that bear his name ; and it was Juan Sebastian del Cano who was the first of these great old seamen to circumnavigate the globe. Upon the races to which such men belonged it seemed that the maritime heritage of the Phœnicians

and of Carthage and Rome, had fallen, and they
drew their instincts and ambitions from the states
of Venice and Genoa, and the schools and harbours
of Portugal and Spain. From them we received
the science and the instruments of the new navigation. The great discoveries they made, with those
of the Dutch, who were before us in the East, and
the enterprises, riches and monopolies that arose
therefrom, were the cause of an astonishing burst
of the spirit of maritime adventure and enterprise
among the seafarers and gentlemen of England. The
exercise of sea power was called for on a much
greater scale, and there resulted an immense development in the seaman's art and craft, which exerted
its influence on shipbuilding, the construction of
better sea-keeping vessels, the development of ports,
and the organization of everything required for the
efficient service of the sea. In the course of events
that succeeded private enterprise and national
endeavour were inextricably confused.

There was a determination to break through
the exclusive commercial policy which the Spaniards
had established in their West Indian possessions,
and men like Drake and Hawkins were not to be
baulked in their search for treasure when it was to
be won at sea. Out of the resolute enterprise of
the Englishmen came the terrible incident of San
Juan de Ulloa, followed by Drake's enterprise of

vengeance, in which he captured Nombre de Dios, sacked Venta Cruz, laid hands on the silver mules of Spanish grandees, and came home with more treasure than ship had ever brought before ; followed also by the famous navigation to the South Sea, in which he captured many a Spanish town and ship, set a girdle about the globe, and came home with treasure, it is said, to the sterling value of a million and a half. To the Spaniards Drake was a pirate who deserved to be hanged, but Elizabeth knighted him and kept the gold. Let this picture suffice to call up the nature of the quarrel, complicated as it was, no doubt, by the favour shown to the rebellious subjects of Spain in the Low Countries, by the efforts of the Spaniards to stir up rebellion in Ireland and by many other things ; embittered too by the religious breach, and by cruelties to English captives in Spain, and to Spanish captives in England.

As to the fleet of Elizabeth's time, it should be noted that it fell very low in the early years of her reign, causing uneasiness for its sufficiency, such as had followed the loss of Calais in her sister's reign. The regeneration began under the impulsion of a commission appointed in 1583, consisting of the high officers of State, including the Lord Admiral, and sub-commissioners of sea experience—Drake, Cotton, Gorges, Frobisher, Bingham, Fulke Greville, Carew, Raleigh, and others—besides the four " principal

officers of our ships "—Wynter, Hawkins, Holstock
and Borough—the chief shipwrights, Pett, Chapman
and Baker, and two chief masters who were
practical navigators. The Mediterranean galley
type of vessel, propelled by oars and with end-on
gun-fire only, was of little value in the ocean ;
the galleasse which attempted to combine broadside fire was unsatisfactory ; and the problem was
to transform the deep-waisted single-decked cog
of the middle ages, with its cage-work and castles
at the bow and stern, as developed in the big ship
of Henry VIII, into a sailing warship of weatherly
character and sea endurance, mounting guns of
greater power on the broadside. How this was
accomplished cannot be told here. The "great
ships" *Triumph* of 1000 tons, carrying thirty-four
30 pounder guns and 16 light guns, the *St Matthew*,
1000 tons, the *White Bear*, 900 tons, and the *Victory*,
Mer Honour and *Ark Royal,* were the biggest ships
of the time.

As to the spirit of the fleet, we know that it had
been won in many a hard-fought battle with the
gale and in hunger and cold. On the great circumnavigation, after the execution of Doughty, Drake
warned his men against mutiny and disagreement.
" For," he said, " I must have the gentleman to
haul and draw with the mariner and the mariner
with the gentleman," and he found none unwilling

"to set his hand to a rope." Howard, waiting for
the Armada, wrote, "There shall be neither sickness nor death which shall make us yield until this
service be ended ; I never saw nobler minds than
be here in our forces." If Drake had had his way,
the Armada would never have reached the Channel.
"With fifty sail of shipping we shall do more good
upon their own coast than a great many more will
do here at home, and the sooner we are gone, the
better we shall be able to impeach them." Hawkins,
Frobisher and Fenner thought with him. It was
in this spirit that Drake had destroyed the shipping
and stores at Cadiz in 1587. The same thought
was in the mind of Raleigh when he would that the
enemy should be busied at home, and before they
could eat of "our Kentish capons."

Elizabeth had nearly 200 vessels of all classes,
with 17,000 or 18,000 men, but by far the greater
number were not fighting ships, and a great many
were not present in the fighting. Although the
Spaniards left the Tagus with 130 ships, it is doubtful if more than 120 ever reached the Channel, with
24,000 men, in a sickly state and ill provided, and
half of the vessels were victuallers, and a great
many pinnaces and small craft. The big ships
were unwieldy, and no match for the more nimble
English vessels. Not many of their men knew the
stormy seas of the North Atlantic ; and most of

them were far inferior to the hardy fellows who had
learned their trade in the Irish and Iceland fisheries,
and had sailed with Frobisher, Davis or Drake.
The Duke of Medina-Sidonia was in command, but
it was against his own will, for, on the death of Santa
Cruz, he had confessed his incompetence, and had
pleaded his ignorance of naval affairs.

The Spanish plan of action was to employ the
Duke of Parma's army in Flanders for the invasion
of England.   The Armada was to bring other troops
in transports, and the English fleet was to be attacked
if met, and brought to close action, so that the
soldiers might play their part, but the principal
object was to get up Channel in order to cover the
movement of Parma's troops from Dunkirk, who
were to cross to England in flat-bottomed boats.
The huge Spanish armament was off the Lizard on
Saturday, the 20th of July, 1588, moving slowly
eastward with a light breeze.   The same afternoon
Howard brought the English fleet out of Plymouth
Sound, and on the next day, having gained the wind
of his adversary, and his ships being better sailers,
fell upon the Spanish rear under Recalde, and so
mauled it, with a rain of shot for three hours, re-
fusing to let the Spaniards approach for close action,
that two great ships were taken.   Still the Englishmen hung on the rear of the speeding Spaniards,
and on the Tuesday there was hard fighting off

Portland. By Thursday the enemy were off the Isle of Wight, where Recalde's ship, the *Santa Ana*, of 768 tons, was so severely damaged that she left the fleet and was run ashore near Havre. Howard, in the *Ark Royal*, husbanded his ammunition, looking for a meeting with the squadron of the Narrow Seas, under Lord Henry Seymour and Sir William Winter. On Saturday afternoon the Spaniards anchored under Cape Grisnez, with the English a mile to windward, and there it was that the reinforcement came. On Sunday night Howard sent fireships amongst the Spaniards, seeing which, in panic, they cut their cables, and drifted in confusion to leeward through the Straits, the English hanging on their rear. The *San Lorenzo* became unmanageable and was captured off Calais, and meanwhile the Armada had arrived off Gravelines.

There, on Monday the 29th of July, was fought the great battle in which the Spaniards were badly beaten, and the whole purpose of their expedition was frustrated. It is impossible to describe the action here. The wings of their half-moon formation were driven in on the centre, where ships fouled one another, and three were sunk and four or five driven ashore. There was great slaughter, and Winter says of the Englishmen, " when every man was weary with labour, and our cartridges spent, and munitions wasted—I think in some altogether—

we ceased, and followed the enemy." The Spanish remnant was retreating along the coast across the estuary of the Thames. " There was never anything pleased me better," wrote Drake, "than to see the enemy flying with a southerly wind to the northward."

The sufferings of the Spaniards in their long navigation were terrible, for their ships were ill-found ; they had been battered by the storms and the English guns ; masts and rigging were shattered ; food and water were scanty and bad. Many ships were lost among the Scottish Islands and on the coast of Ireland, and probably few of the vessels that went north-about ever returned to Spain. There had been hardships in the English ships also, and there was sickness which the men attributed to sour beer, and the food was insufficient and bad. That, however, was too often the seaman's lot.

The defeat of the Invincible Armada—that description was not official, for the real title was " Felicisima Armada "—was one of the decisive battles of the world. It not only once more pro-tected England from invasion ; it put an end to Spanish domination at sea, and removed the first obstacle to the exercise of British influence and ultimately the exertion of British power through the world. The Spaniards had sought to make the sea a pathway to their conquest, but they had found it a barrier to their ambition.

This chapter may well close with a reference to the heroic fight of gallant Grenville in the *Revenge* against outnumbering Spanish foes at the Azores in 1591—a fight which showed the ardour and mettle of our seamen, but which, as seamen know, was useless to the English cause, and a sacrifice which cooler judgment would hardly have approved.

CHAPTER VI

THE TRANSITION NAVY.   TUDORS AND STUARTS

THE defeat of the Armada, though ultimately it proved a most damaging blow to Spain, had not brought to Elizabeth the immediate objects she desired. She but dimly realized that a new world had been discovered, and that her seamen were breaking down the barriers by which its treasures were withheld. She did not regard the Fleet as an instrument to be used for what might be called imperial purposes. It was her view or hope that the operations in the Low Countries and France would sap the life-blood of Spain, and Parma's invasion of France in 1590 had entangled Philip in another long and wasting war. She had asked her seamen in 1588 how many Spanish ships had been boarded, how much treasure had been captured,

and how many prisoners taken ; on which matters
neither the Lord Admiral nor Drake had been able
to give very satisfactory answers. Had not the
main body of the Armada escaped to the northward,
and might it not refit in Denmark, and return ?
Such doubts and apprehensions as these had dis-
quieted the Queen, and her disappointment influenced her policy. The expedition of Drake and
Norreys to Lisbon, in retaliation for the Armada,
failed in some of its objects, and was marred by the
disagreements of its leaders. The enterprises to
the " Isles " for the interception of Spanish supplies,
and the great stroke intended for the capture of
the enemy's treasure at Panama in 1595–6, during
which expedition Hawkins and Drake died, as well
even as Essex's attack on Cadiz—the famous Cadiz
voyage—in 1596, did not produce the pecuniary
results desired—for plunder was at that time an
object of war—and they revealed disagreements
between the chiefs, and quarrels between seamen
and soldiers which marked the gradually growing
and necessary ascendancy of the former.

But in effect the pressure of sea control, and the
wasting canker in the Low Countries had together
created a sore situation in Spain, and the treasury
was empty. The cities, however, were patriotic,
and Philip, sitting at the Council table, exclaimed,
" We will sell these candlesticks if other means of

raising money cannot be found ! " The Spanish menace accordingly continued for several years. There was a new threat in 1597 ; the Spaniards were well established on the Brittany coast ; and in 1601 Spanish soldiers, to the number of 3500, were even landed in Ireland to assist Tyrone. Meanwhile Elizabeth, declaring that she would do only what was necessary for defence, had not properly defended Ireland, and was trusting to her diplomacy and waiting for successes to be won vicariously by the Dutch and French on the continent. Yet exhaustion was falling upon both countries, and ultimately it paralysed the power of Spain.

The real note of the period was the presence of the English flag in every sea. Colonists were establishing themselves on the coasts of North America, and before Elizabeth died, in 1603, merchants were preparing to dispute with the Dutch the rich promise of the eastern trade.

The reign of James I was undistinguished in the annals of the Navy, though it was a period of great importance. The old order had passed away, and the fleet of James was a fleet divided into rates, controlled on a system that still exists. The period saw the King's ships employed in the keeping of the vague area known as the " Narrow Seas," or the " Four Seas," by means of a " Summer Guard " and sometimes a " Winter Guard." It was a maritime

truce, during which new antagonisms were coming
into being. The English claim to the sovereignty
of the seas by the exaction of a salute as homage to
the flag, was becoming ever more irksome to the
Dutch. Their shipping was growing in volume,
and they feared a quarrel while they were still
embroiled with Spain. They were willing to show
respect, but they deeply resented anything that
might imply inferiority. Peace was also the great
desire of James, and the enterprise in 1614, of
Sir William Monson and Sir Francis Howard against
the pirates who infested the Scottish coasts was in
pursuance of the peace of the seas, as was Sir Robert
Mansel's expedition of 1620 against the Algerine
pirates. The latter was futile, but showed a new
spirit in the despatch of the King's ships for the
protection of foreign trade.

Shipbuilding entered upon a new development
in James's reign by the building of the *Prince Royal*,
in 1610, being a two-decked ship with quarter-deck
and forecastle, which, stripped of the lavish carvings
that adorned her, resembled generally the ships
built up to the close of the 18th century. Her
designer was the celebrated Phineas Pett, son of
Elizabeth's shipwright at Deptford, but she was
thought unsatisfactory, and a survey showed that
she had been built of unseasoned wood, whereby
after a few years she became useless for the service.

Experience, however, had been gained during her construction, and in the next reign Pett attained great success with the famous *Sovereign of the Seas*, built in 1637, which was the first three-decker in the Navy. Though good work was done, it was too evident that the administration of the dockyards had become exceedingly corrupt. An inquiry in 1608 had laid bare the evils, but little had been done to amend them. Howard, the Lord High Admiral, was too old to welcome reform and the service was afflicted with every disease that could infect a navy. Ten years later, however, Buckingham having now succeeded Howard, the Board of Principal Officers was dissolved, and a businesslike Council of Commissioners, after inquiry, carried on the work, purified to some extent the dockyard administration, and built two ships each year for five consecutive years. Ten years later again, in 1628, the Principal Officers were once more raised to authority.

Flagrant corruption, waste, neglect and the decay of maritime enterprise exercised a disastrous effect in the reign of Charles I, and this is true although, like all the Stuarts, he had a full sense of the importance of maritime ascendancy in the presence of the growing power of continental states. The Navy was still in a transition stage, depending much upon the mercantile marine, and the merchants came unwillingly. There was the long quarrel with the

Parliament, and the King never had money enough for his purposes. Sir John Mervyn, commanding in the Narrow Seas, described the deplorable state of the ships in 1629, in which men were ill fed and mutinous, while their petitions to Parliament remained unread. " His majesty will lose the honour of his seas, the love and loyalty of his sailors, and his royal navy will droop." When the miserable expedition returned from Cadiz four years earlier, Sir John Pennington reported that most of the seamen were sick or dead. St Leger wrote " they stink as they go, and the poor rags they have are rotten and ready to fall off." Mervyn recorded that " foul weather, naked bodies and empty bellies made the seamen voice the King's service worse than galley slavery."

There is little of interest to detain us in the expeditions and cruises of Charles's reign, though to that period may be traced the first movements tending towards the establishment of our naval position in the Mediterranean. Ship money was an experiment which proved a disaster to the Crown, and the Ship Money Fleet, though built to assert our claim to the sovereignty of the Narrow Seas, was not well employed for that purpose. Possibly, however, it exercised a deterrent influence upon the ambitions of Holland and France, and gave time for the administrative reorganization of the Navy.

But it was not able to protect the national honour, when the famous Dutch admiral, Marten Harpertsz Tromp, in our own waters, defeated the Spaniards in contemptuous disregard of a squadron which Pennington had at Dover. The fleet which Charles had built proved, indeed, the immediate cause of his ruin. It went over to the Parliament, and remained an instrument in the hands of his enemies until, in 1648, a part of it revolted and was carried over to Helvoetsluys, and placed by some of the best men in the service at the disposal of the Prince of Wales. What part the Commonwealth Navy played in the Second Civil War cannot be related here.

CHAPTER VII

THE NEW CONTEST FOR DOMINION.
THE FIRST DUTCH WAR

In all this history, to use the words of John Hollond, in his *Brief Discourse of the Navy*, 1638, " the naval part is the thread that runs through the whole wooft, the burden of the song, the scope of the text." What was true of the years before 1638 was more true of many years that followed. The men who laid hands on power when Charles was dead were men of a new mould, who gave a fresh impress to the Navy, and some new vigour, though they could not remove all abuses. The marvellous cruises and high courage of Prince Rupert and his companions, first near home, and then in the Mediterranean and the Atlantic, encountering or eluding in succession Blake, Deane, Ayscue and Penn (1649–1653) showed the seamanlike qualities which were the great endowment of Englishmen, whether Roundheads or Cavaliers.

The fleet of the Commonwealth learned much of its business in the chase of Rupert, which carried Penn into the Mediterranean in 1651, being the first English admiral since the Crusades to enter those waters with any other object than the repression of piracy. Blake, Popham and Deane, appointed Admirals and Generals at Sea in February, 1649, were soon discovered, with their comrades, using the Fleet with vigour and skill, and giving wholesome lessons thereby to Portuguese, Spaniards, Dutch and French ; while crushing out the remnants of Royalist opposition. And yet Blake, an Oxford scholar, merchant, politician and army Colonel, had never been at sea before the age of fifty. The first object of the Commonwealth leaders had been to set the administration in better order, and it was brought under an Admiralty Committee of the Parliament, with a Navy Board, which consisted of the Treasurer, Surveyor, Comptroller and Clerk of the Acts who conducted the civil business. These bodies

worked zealously, and by the year 1651, the strength
of the Navy had practically been doubled. The
fidelity of the officers was secured by appointing
trusted men, and the content of the men by placing
over them officers after their own heart, and by
better pay, better food and better prize-money, with
much improved administration in home matters.
At the same time the organization of the Fleet was
advanced towards the making of a permanent force,
and the fleet tactics were put upon a new basis.
Efforts had been made in earlier years to formulate
tactical systems, but they were rudimentary, and
orders issued in 1653 for the line ahead formation,
which has since been used in all our wars and still
endures, were clearly based on previous experience
in the service.

Howard, writing in June, 1588, had laid down
a great strategic principle—not, however, as we
have seen in a previous chapter, new with him—
that he would not go to any place to offend or to
spoil, " but to seek out the great force and to fight
with them." This ruling principle began to receive its real exemplification in the Dutch Wars,
which were not conducted by the adventures of
single ships or small forces, but by steady coherent
campaigns. The wars with the United Provinces
were inevitable. Raleigh could remember, when one
of Elizabeth's ships would " make forty Hollanders

strike sail and come to an anchor," but now we were to see how unwilling were they to submit to our power. Their prosperity, like our own, was founded upon commerce. From a race of herring-fishers they had become a ruling mercantile power in the world. They had preceded us in oversea trade and, displacing the Portuguese, had founded a great colonial dominion, even while they were holding their own against all the armaments of Spain. It was the massacre at Amboyna in 1623 that drove back our traders on the Indian continent, and thus indirectly led to the foundation of the Indian Empire. Thus the wars with the Dutch were commercial wars, and in a volume which is concerned with the influence of the Navy on the growth of Empire, it is important to lay stress on this fact. The commercial character of the hostilities was indicated by the Navigation Act of 1651, which was intended to strike hard at the Dutch carrying trade. There had as yet arisen no instinct for the use of the fleet as a political instrument. The objects were direct and practical.

The immediate cause of the outbreak was the state of undeclared hostilities which existed between France and England, Dutch ships, as neutrals, being searched, sometimes harshly treated by our captains, and subjected to a law of prize which was not their own. In May, 1652, Tromp with some

forty sail, was in the Straits of Dover, awaiting
valuable Dutch convoys which were coming up
Channel. He had no desire to bring about a conflict, but was quite ready for one. Off the Start
certain of the Dutch ships had been compelled to
strike their flags after a fight with Captain Young,
commanding the "West Guard," and it was hardly
likely that if Tromp met the Englishmen, they
would part without a battle. Rear-Admiral Bourne
was in the Downs with eight sail and Blake at Wye
with fifteen or sixteen. Tromp had orders to protect
the convoy, which had reached Fairlight, and on
May 19th Blake, seeing the Dutchmen bearing down
towards him, Tromp leading in the *Brederode*,
thought they had "a resolution to engage." There
is a dispute as to which side fired the first broadside.
Tromp had the weather gage, that is the wind
behind him, and he made a fierce attack on Blake's
ship, the *James*, which was the weathermost of the
squadron. The battle raged for two hours, Tromp's
rear being engaged by Bourne, who came out from
the Downs, but the gunnery was ineffective, and
Tromp, though in overwhelming superiority, withdrew.

This action caused a strong outburst of feeling
in both countries, and every available ship was
made ready for the coming struggle. Early in July
Blake was in the North Sea with fifty sail, preying

upon the Dutch herring-fleets, by which the whole fishery was lost for a year, and looking for Dutch Indiamen coming north-about round Scotland, while Ayscue was in the Downs with fifteen or sixteen sail waiting for shipping from the Thames. Tromp, with a great fleet, made no attempt to protect the fisheries and failed to bring Ayscue to action, after which he went north to seek Blake, but was driven to his ports by storms. The gallant old officer had done ill in this business, and was compelled to relinquish his charge.

The attack and protection of commerce was the main concern of the admirals, and De Ruyter and Ayscue were both sent down Channel with this object. A collision occurred on August 16th, which was inconclusive, but De Ruyter carried off his convoy, eluding also Blake and Penn, who had come down Channel, and the Dutch object of getting their shipping home was attained. The Battle of the Kentish Knock, fought on September 27th outside the Thames, between Blake and Penn on the one side and Cornelius De With and De Ruyter on the other, was the first action of the war not directly concerned with the protection of convoys. It was inconclusive ; but the Dutch had the worst of it. They did not fight well, and some of the captains behaved very badly, being apparently supporters of Tromp, unwilling to support De With and De

Ruyter. The Dutch now prepared a great armament, and recalled Tromp to the command, as the
man of experience who inspired confidence. Tromp
got his huge convoy, about 400 sail, through the
Straits, and off Dungeness on November 30th,
having 80 ships to 40, inflicted a reverse upon Blake,
who was severely handled and lost two vessels.

This lesson was taken to heart, and a great fleet
of 70 or 80 ships, with Blake, Deane and Monk
executing the office of Lord High Admiral in command at sea, was in the Channel in February, 1653,
and on the 18th again encountered Tromp, who had
80 or 90 men-of-war, and a cloud of merchantmen
behind him. The battle lasted three days and
extended from Portland to the Straits of Dover.
On the first day, the English were severely handled ;
the second day's fighting was inconclusive ; but on
the third day, in a close action, Penn, off Cape Grisnez,
broke through Tromp's formation, and several men-
of-war and some 50 merchantmen were captured.
The Dutch admiral showed fine seamanship in escaping, and the action was really indecisive, for the
bulk of the convoy reached the Dutch ports. Both
Blake and Deane were wounded, there were heavy
losses among officers and seamen, and the victorious
fleet was reduced to a condition scarcely more battle-
worthy than that of its adversary.

But from this time onward superiority rested

with the Englishmen. Their ships were better
than the Dutch ships, and the men fought better.
There was greater skill also in the handling of fleets.
Operations were not resumed until May, 1653,
and on June 2nd and 3rd Deane and Monk, with
over 80 sail were once more engaged with Tromp
off the Gabbard Shoal outside the Thames. Seeing
his danger the latter accepted battle to leeward, so
that he could escape, which he did, keeping in the
shallows of the Flemish coast and reaching his
harbours. In this action there were severe losses,
and Deane was cut in two by a cannon shot in the
first broadside, but the defeat of the Dutch was
complete. This misfortune, which spread consterna-
tion throughout the United Provinces, was due in
no measure to lack of courage or skill, but to the
inferiority of the Dutch ships, concerning which
Tromp had protested to the States General. Out-
spoken as he always was, De With exclaimed, " The
English are at present masters of us and of the seas."
So dire was the situation that the Dutch sought
peace, but Cromwell's terms were too harsh, and
the States General would not submit to conditions
which were thought an outrage.

Thus came to be fought the last fight of the war,
the famous battle of 1653 off the Texel, in which
Monk was in command with Penn and Lawson as
his colleagues. The Fleet had been kept off the

Dutch coasts, engaged effectively in the new work of blockade. It is impossible to describe the desperate fight of July 31st, which was conducted with the utmost fierceness and with heavy losses on both sides. The greatest loss of all to the Dutch was that of Tromp who was stricken down early in the action, and was succeeded by Evertsen. " If they should cast twenty John Evertsens and twenty De Ruyters into one," said a writer of the time, " they could not make one Tromp." There was no shrinkage from action in this battle, no convoy to protect, and all that courage and skill could do for Holland was done, but the English victory was decisive. The Dutch were inferior in ships and crews, and most of all in discipline and fighting power. They again sued for peace, which was finally agreed upon some months later.

There was other fighting in this war, especially between Badiley and Van Galen in the Mediterranean, but it cannot be described here. We will, however, observe certain points which are of importance. In the early stage of the war, the idea of seeking out and destroying the enemy's main fleet, which became later the cardinal principle of strategy, had scarcely been conceived. Everything turned upon the protection of convoy. As the hostilities progressed, the truer object of war necessarily emerged. Then we must note the growing weakness of the Dutch, who had been wasted by land warfare, and also the increasing sense in England of the need of higher fighting organization, and the building of the right classes of ships for admirals to handle. Next we may remark the advantage resulting to this country in the war from undivided organization and direction, as contrasted with the divided counsels and divergent interests of the United Provinces. Lastly we may see the effect of the war—the striking of what promised to be a mortal blow at the prosperity of the Netherlands. The British Isles, by their geographical situation, were seated, as it were, athwart the Dutch lines of communications, and by exerting the compression of sea power, as Admiral Mahan has said, the Fleet " caused the grass to grow in the streets of Amsterdam."

CHAPTER VIII

THE RESTORATION NAVY AND THE CLOSE OF THE DUTCH WARS

WE are confronted, when we reach the Navy of the Restoration, with a contrast between administrative wisdom on the one hand and the effects of administrative failure on the other. Before Charles

landed at Dover, he appointed as Lord High Admiral,
his brother James, Duke of York, afterwards James II,
whose name will always be remembered with those
of our greatest naval administrators. The large
committee appointed by the Rump Parliament to
manage the affairs of the Navy was swept away,
and the four " Principal Officers " were restored—
Sir George Carteret, the Treasurer, a sea-officer of
great experience fully trusted, and, says Pepys, " a
most honest man " ; the Comptroller, Sir Robert
Slyngesbie, who from his childhood had been bred
up and employed in the Navy ; the Surveyor,
Sir William Batten, who had held the same office
before, and had served in active commands ; and
the Clerk of the Acts, Samuel Pepys himself, the
Diarist, whose Diary covers but a very small period
of his long and active service for the State. With
them were associated three commissioners, all men
of experience, and their successors were men of
experience also. These officers came to be called
the Navy Board, acting as the Lord High Admiral's
council of advice, and the Board continued to exist
as a Board long afterwards, when the office of Lord
High Admiral had been placed in Commission in
the hands of the Board of Admiralty. A great work
was rapidly accomplished in firmly establishing the
code of naval discipline, and the Duke applied
himself particularly to the better ordering of the

" Œconomy " of the Navy Office and the constitution of an organized corps of naval officers.

Notwithstanding all the experience brought to
bear upon the business, deep disappointment
followed. " Back again to Spring Garden," wrote
Pepys, on the 3rd of June, 1667, " and then to
walk up and down the garden, reflecting upon the
bad management of things now, compared with
what it was in the late rebellious times, when men,
some for fear, and some for religion, minded their
business, which none now do, by being void of both."
No one knew better than Pepys that want of money
was at the root of the administrative failure, and
that the evil of private gain at the country's cost
seemed incurable. When the King came back the
situation had been deplorable. The Navy was even
then overwhelmed with debt, and the requirements
were ever increasing, and outgrowing the administrative machinery. During the Second Dutch War
the evil fruit ripened. " Did business, though not
much at the office " ; wrote Pepys, 7th October,
1665, after the first battles, " because of the horrible
crowd and lamentable moan of the poor seamen
that lie starving in the streets for lack of money."
With the remark that as time passed on, good administrative means began to bear better fruit, with
amendment at the dockyards and in the service, we
pass on to this new war with the Dutch, premising

that the Fleet was employed in 1662–3, against the Barbary pirates, and in taking possession of Tangier, part of the dowry of Catherine of Braganza.

The Second Dutch War, 1665–7, arose from the old commercial rivalry, embittered by political exasperation. The English, as Monk frankly said, " wanted a larger share in the trade of the Dutch," which had greatly increased since the previous war, mainly owing to the anti-Spanish operations of Cromwell, which had thrown the Spanish trade into their hands. The chartered trading companies, by their rivalries, contributed to the unfriendliness; in the Mediterranean, Sir John Lawson, co-operating against the pirates with De Ruyter, had exacted a salute which he had refused to return; and in his well known cruise of 1663, Sir Robert Holmes had dealt in a very hostile manner with the Dutch possessions on the West Coast of Africa and at New Amsterdam. The significant feature of the war that followed was that the Dutch abandoned their trade in order to fight for the essential command of the sea. The fleets were organized on a great scale, and, in May, 1665, the Duke of York, with nearly a hundred sail, having with him Penn, Prince Rupert and Sandwich, stretched over to the Dutch coast but failed to force an action, and returned. The Dutch had been unprepared, but they were soon at sea, and Opdam, with reluctance due to a sense

4—2

of inferiority, came over with a large fleet, which was severely beaten in the battle off Lowestoft (3rd June). Serious losses were inflicted on the English ships in this action, especially among the highly placed officers in immediate attendance upon the Duke in the *Royal Charles.* The Earls of Marlborough and Falmouth, Sir John Lawson, perhaps the most ardent spirit in the fleet, Admiral Sansum and Lord Muskerry were amongst the slain, a fact which may account for the Duke's failure to pursue his enemy. Some of the Dutch captains had behaved very badly, and four of them were afterwards shot. Probably their misconduct was largely instrumental in Opdam's failure, for his material losses did not exceed about fifteen sail. De Ruyter was now the only man whom the Dutch could trust, and Sandwich, in the North Sea, let him slip by as he returned from a long cruise to the West Indies greatly encumbered with the prizes in his company.

The English fleet was in a bad state. It was ill provided, pay was in arrear and the victualling service was disorganized. With great difficulty a fleet of some eighty-five sail was assembled in the Downs in May, 1666, under command of Monk, for Sandwich was discredited, while Rupert was in the Channel looking for the French, who, it was feared, would join the Dutch. De Ruyter, with Cornelis

Evertsen and the younger Tromp, came over in greatly superior force, and on June 1st the hard-fought four days' battle of the Straits of Dover began. The *Swiftsure*, Sir William Berkeley's flagship, was cut off and captured, the admiral being killed. Out of the struggle broke gallant Sir John Harman, giving proof of grim and dauntless courage, when deeply wounded, with his ship on fire and his crew in a panic.

The second day's fighting was inconclusive, and once more there was misconduct amongst the Dutch captains. The English had shown themselves superior in manœuvring and fighting power, but were outnumbered, and on the third day Monk found it necessary to retire to the Thames to make good damage. The Dutch followed, and captured the *Prince*, Sir George Ayscue's flagship, which had stranded on the Galloper Sand. Fortunately, at the moment, Rupert, who had been anxiously awaited, appeared off the Foreland, whereupon the Dutch made sail with their prize. But on the next day valiant Monk was again at sea, and in a fight which lasted many hours, his fleet got the worst of it, but not without inflicting such damage upon De Ruyter's ships that he could make no immediate use of his success, and was obliged to retire to his ports to refit.

There was evidence in all that had taken place,

with abundant courage in the few and even in very many, of a decline in the moral quality of the English Fleet, and of the nation behind it. The pages of Pepys's Diary bear evidence of an ominous change. Yet in the last battle of the war, in a burst of shameful resentment at what had occurred, a new spirit was created, De Ruyter was forced from the station which he had assumed at the mouth of the Thames, and Monk and Rupert crossed to the Dutch coast, driving shipping to shelter and capturing prizes, while the operation known as " Sir Robert Holmes his Bonefire " recalls how Holmes burned 160 sail of merchantmen and two warships at Terschelling (August 8th), and captured stores and destroyed magazines, to the total value, it is said, of well over a million sterling.

But the Dutch were neither beaten nor cowed, and with stubborn courage within a month were at sea again, looking for a junction with the French fleet, which Rupert forestalled. The immediate danger passed away, but the moral weakness and decay alluded to asserted itself afresh. Penury reduced Charles's fleet to impotence, and the cup of shame was filled when the Dutch under De Ruyter and Van Ghent entered the Thames and captured and burned the ships at Chatham. Seven large ships burned or taken, with many smaller, were the toll of the Dutch success, and long after the event

at Chatham, De Ruyter remained master of Thames'
mouth and the south-eastern coasts of England.

Peace was signed at Breda, but it was of short
duration. Though the war was disliked in England,
the Dutch were still rivals too formidable to be
allowed to exist, and Sir Robert Holmes, therefore,
without declaration of war, was sent, in 1671, to
intercept the Dutch Smyrna convoy. There was a
sharp fight in the Channel, in which one Dutch warship and several merchantmen were captured, but the
English ships were roughly handled, and to the
King's disappointment most of the intended prizes
escaped. War was declared in March, 1672. The
French were then our allies, for the Dutch had
opposed the conquest of the Spanish Netherlands.
Vice-Admiral Count d'Estrées was sent with a force
which constituted the white squadron in the Battle
of Solebay (Southwold), the 28th of May. This
squadron fell to leeward, and was held in check by the
Dutch admiral Bankert, while De Ruyter delivered a
furious attack on the English fleet, himself singling
out the *Prince*, which was the Duke of York's flagship. She was terribly mauled, as was the *St Michael*,
to which the Duke transferred his flag. The Earl of
Sandwich gallantly perished in his flagship, the *Royal
James*, and Van Ghent, who attacked him was shot in
the heat of the battle. It was a furious fight, in
which De Ruyter obtained the victory, though his

own forces suffered almost as severely. The last action of the war was the hard-fought Battle of the Texel, August 11th, 1673, which was not a victory for our arms.

The Dutch admiral had once more saved his country by his courage, foresight and tactical skill. But the United Provinces could no longer hold their place amid the growing power of their neighbours. As with the Spaniards before them, their life-blood was wasting in an exhausting struggle on land. They had clung too long to the friendship of France ; but Louis never forgave their resistance in the Spanish Netherlands, and when his armies marched the glare of its watch-fires was seen even in Amsterdam. Then arose the old stubborn spirit, and William of Orange, who became Stadholder after the assassination of De Witt, won province after province back from the French. But the burden was too great, and, if the Revolution of 1688, which was to make the Dutch our friends, had not taken place, they could never have held their position at sea in the presence of the growing power and resources of England.

But in England the malady of decay, the terrible waste due to want of money and want of credit, reduced the Navy to a shameful degree at the close of Charles's reign. Yet there had been many actions that illuminated its story. The operations of

Harman in the West Indies, of Munden at St Helena, and of others on the coasts of India and elsewhere, showed how the building of empire was going on. Much of the Dutch trade fell into our hands. Tangier had been occupied, and Rooke, Marlborough, Shovell and others had shown the true qualities of our seamen in the Mediterranean. Tangier, however, that outpost of power, at one of the gates of the world, was abandoned in the impotence of 1684.

CHAPTER IX

THE REVOLUTION OF 1688. THE BEGINNING OF THE FRENCH WARS

IT will have been observed in the preceding chapters that the removal of the Spaniards and the Dutch from the pathways of our enterprise and our approaches to the position of a World Power, was not brought about by the great engagements and actions of the Navy in the wars. No battle we have mentioned can in a real sense be spoken of as decisive. It cannot be said that the defeat of the Armada in 1588 reduced Spain to the impotence to which she subsequently fell. No battle of the Dutch wars brought about the decay of the Dutch Republic. We must rather trace the causes of

these changes in the relative positions of nations to
the all-pervading pressure of sea-power, not always
nor merely by the direct gripping of the avenues
of commerce or communications, but often by
the exhaustion which results from the wasting of
resources, the material and personal losses, the
destruction of industries, and convulsions in the
social state, called up by the loud voices of Faction
and Want. These things affected England as they
did Spain and the Netherlands, and their consequences were disastrous for the social state; but
we had not to bear the double burden of land and
sea, and we did not maintain great standing armies,
conduct vast military campaigns, or empty our
resources in covering the land with mighty fortresses
and entrenched camps. Here was the real cause
of our endurance of what others could not bear.
The fleets had protected us from invasion, and opened
the seas for us, and we were free to pursue alike our
industries within and our activities without.

Nevertheless, at the close of the reign of Charles I
the King was at the end of his resources, and few
ships were in commission; the rest were out of
repair, and the magazines were almost empty.
James II therefore appointed a commission to
inquire into the affairs of the Navy, which conducted its work until October, 1688. Much was
done for the betterment of the service, but not all

the defects resulting from years of corruption could
be removed. Yet at the close of the period, there
existed an establishment of 173 vessels, including
9 first-rates, 11 second-rates and 39 third-rates,
besides 26 fireships and three yachts. Sir Roger
Strickland had a squadron of 20 sail in the Downs,
which was strengthened and placed under command
of Lord Dartmouth. The new menace from the
Netherlands was discerned, and the Prince of Orange
was expected to attempt a landing. We all know
how that landing took place. It was not due to the
inability of an efficient and resolute Navy to prevent invasion, but to the treason of officers and the
acquiescence of men who did not desire to avert
but to bring about the Revolution which put an
end to the Stuart dynasty.

The fleet which James had assembled, and the
system he had created were a valuable possession
for his successor. But the new King was a soldier,
who came looking for military objects, and regarded the Navy as a means for their immediate·
accomplishment. He showed no large understanding of sea power, until later when he discerned
that it must be the chief agency in the diplomacy
of his grouping of the nations. His accession,
while it made the Dutch our allies, opened on a
larger scale our secular hostility to France, and
ultimately brought Spain and the House of Austria

into a coalition against Louis XIV, which laid the foundation of the new Grand Alliance. William's immediate objects were to secure the Narrow Seas, for invasion was an imminent danger, and to maintain communications with Ireland, which had to be conquered from James, who had been landed in the island by French ships under Gabaret. That the naval danger existed was shown by Châteaurenault's success in landing a small body of troops at Bantry Bay in despite of a squadron under command of Herbert, afterwards Earl of Torrington, an honour that officer received in recognition of this, the first naval action of the new reign.

Louis' real object was to secure such command of the sea as would prepare the way for invasion, and thereby bring about a rising for the restoration of the Stuarts. The great minister Colbert had provided and organized the Navy, and that fine seaman Tourville was charged with the operation. Torrington was in command of the fleet which was to frustrate the attempt. At the Admiralty he had protested against its insufficiency, and afloat, knowing his inferiority, he desired to pursue a policy of observation, and to keep his fleet " in being " rather than to suffer defeat, which would imperil the safety of the country and probably the stability of the throne. Torrington's action has been the subject of a good deal of discussion. His ideas were prevalent at the time both in the French navy and in our own. They resulted from experience of the sailing navy in times when fleets could not keep the seas in all weathers, and when, if they could be maintained without encountering the enemy, they might win time for reinforcement for a later campaign. Queen Mary, acting as regent, or her advisers, amongst whom was Russell, Torrington's professional rival, objected however to his policy, and peremptory orders were issued to him to fight. Thus was brought about the Battle of Beachy Head, 30th June, 1690, wherein the Dutch van under Evertsen suffered severely, being first engaged, and Torrington, having, as he considered, carried out his instructions, and knowing he had no chance of success, withdrew to the Thames, as Monk had done before him, though in different circumstances. He was tried by court martial for his failure and acquitted. The battle was reckoned a victory by the French.

The consequences Torrington feared did not immediately follow, but Louis gained great confidence from the success, and in the next year Tourville made, under instructions, what is known as his " campagne au large," in which he was not to fight, but to keep his fleet intact, to protect French interests and the coasts, and if possible to capture

the Smyrna convoy. He was forbidden to enter
the Channel. In the following year, 1692, all was
considered ready for the great expedition against
England. The soldiers had spoken the last word,
and it was for the Navy to carry out their behests.
Precisely the same situation arose a century later,
when other soldiers were ready for a like enterprise. Troops to the number of 20,000 were en-
camped near La Hougue, under command of
Marshal de Bellefonds, with whom was King James,
and cavalry and artillery were to be embarked at
Havre. But Colbert had died, and his successor
Seignelay was less than half-hearted in the duties
of his office. His record shows that he had no
appreciation of the essentials of sea power, and he
relinquished the affairs of the expedition into the
hands of King James, Bellefonds and the soldiers.
Tourville's list shows that he had only forty-four
sail with his flag. Prudence would have counselled waiting for reinforcements which D'Estrées,
Châteaurenault and De la Porte could have brought,
raising the number of ships to eighty-eight. But
Tourville was allowed no discretion, and was condemned to play a rôle in an operation which, he
said, took account neither of naval nor military
difficulties. The King's caution of the previous
year had vanished. Tourville was very willing to
fight the allies, but had no relish for a rash

enterprise. Like Torrington he would have liked to await the preparation of a larger fleet, and meanwhile to keep his fleet " in being," and like Queen Mary, King Louis would have none of his caution, and issued orders that he must fight however strong his opponents might be—*en quelque nombre qu'ils soient*. We thus observe how in both countries soldiers and politicians overrode naval opinion and even common discretion, and we see the danger of such a method of conducting national affairs.

The allied fleet was under command of Admiral Edward Russell, with whom were Sir Ralph Delaval, Sir Cloudesley Shovell, Sir George Rooke and other admirals, and in company were two Dutch squadrons constituting a total strength of 99 vessels. The opposing forces were in view of one another on the 19th May off Cape Barfleur. Tourville, who was to windward, gave orders to attack, and bore down upon the centre of the line. A fierce fight ensued, in which the *Soleil Royal*, his flagship, was seriously damaged. The admiral, like Torrington in 1690, had carried out his instructions, and hoping he had crippled his adversaries, made sail to the westward in a fog which had stopped the firing. There was very little wind, but the fog lifted and his movement was discovered. Fortunately for Russell he had with him, in the captain and master of the fleet, David Mitchell and John Benbow, seamen from boyhood, who well knew the tides and half tides round the French coast. The opposing fleets drifted westward with the tide and anchored when it was against them, and on the morning of the 21st a number of the French ships rounded Cape de la Hague, and ultimately found shelter at St Malo. The *Soleil Royal* and two other crippled ships had not weathered the Cape and were driven ashore and burned near Cherbourg by Sir Ralph Delaval.

Other French ships failing to anchor were driven eastward before the wind between the shore and the allies, and rounding Cape Barfleur, sought refuge in the harbour of Saint Vaast de la Hougue. There, in attacks with boats and fireships, under the conduct of Rooke, on the 22nd and 23rd, thirteen ships were destroyed. The long-drawn action thus ended in brilliant fashion, and nothing of a like kind occurred for many long years to follow. There were great rejoicings in England, for had not the fleet saved the country from invasion once more ? Peace was signed in October, 1697.

Between this period and the Peace of Utrecht, 1713, there was a great deal of fighting which shall not detain us here. Attacks which we had made on the French Channel ports did little to affect the situation. Tourville's exploit against the great convoy at Lagos on the coast of Portugal, had struck dismay in the hearts of London merchants. Much might be written concerning the King's policy in the Mediterranean. New combinations had arisen, and the great Sea Power began to make her influence felt on the states bordering the basin of old-world dominion. War was declared afresh in 1702, and an attack on Cadiz failed owing to dissensions between seamen and soldiers. The capture of Gibraltar by Rooke and Shovell in 1704 gave us one of the great strategic keys of the world, in the very year in which the victory of Blenheim detached the Bavarians from the alliance with France ; and in the sanguinary battle of Malaga nothing was accomplished to restore it to Spain. Four years later Leake took Sardinia and Minorca, with the valuable harbour of Port Mahon. We were thus as strongly based in the western Mediterranean as either France or Spain, and the French fleet did not dare to leave Toulon.

The most significant feature of the war was indeed the progressive exhaustion of France, which, combined with the unenlightenment of her Ministers, brought about the withdrawal of her fleets from the sea. It was the golden age of the great privateers, but Jean Bart, Duguay-Trouin and the rest, do what damage they might to commerce by their brilliant deeds, could neither decrease the strain that was strangling France, nor affect the result of the war.

If it were necessary to make a catalogue of gallant
actions in our own service, we might think of Hop-
sonn breaking the boom at Vigo, 1702, of Benbow
valiantly fighting against Du Casse, but abandoned
by his captains in the same year, and of other hard-
fighting seamen. The betrayal of Benbow by his
captains is evidence of a moral failure in the fleet of
which something shall yet be said.

In this remarkable period, the fleets of the
alliance cruised unchecked, and hemmed France in,
injuring her coasts, annihilating her commerce at
sea, and rendering aid to the armies operating
against her. Squadrons were sent out year by year
to attack French possessions in the New World
and to defend our own. It was the period in which
the foundations of our world-empire, laid a century
before, were strengthened and deepened, and as
Mahan has written of the War of the Spanish Succession, " Before that war England was one of the
Sea Powers ; after it she was *the* Sea Power without any exception."

CHAPTER X

NAVAL SUPREMACY AND FLEET DECAY

THE Peace of Utrecht is one of the great
landmarks in European history. It affected an
astonishing aggrandisement of the position of
England in Europe, gave her commercial supremacy,
and opened wider way for her polity and trade in
the New World. It marked, as the war which it
closed had determined, the decay of her ancient
rival, who had been her ally in the war. From
Spain we retained Gibraltar, Port Mahon and the
Isle of Minorca, and obtained the valuable privilege
called the " Asiento," or right to supply negro slaves
to the Spanish possessions in America, as well as
authority to send a ship laden with manufactured
goods once a year to the Spanish Main. France
surrendered to us Nova Scotia, Newfoundland and
the Hudson's Bay Territory. The Dutch were
deeply mortified at the result. The Spanish Netherlands had been saved from the hand of France, but
there was no share for them in the " Asiento," or
at Gibraltar or Port Mahon. They had, however,
taken no active part in the Mediterranean since
1706, and no heed was paid to their abstract claims
for colonies or stations. Through sheer exhaustion
they were declining. Their navy was shrinking

from want of resources to maintain it, and they gradually withdrew from the wars and the diplomacy of Europe.

Although it would be impossible to estimate the relative weight of the several factors—naval, military, economic and social—which gave us the supremacy we had attained, we may say with certainty, in the words of John Hollond, quoted in a previous chapter, that the naval part was the thread that ran through the whole " wooft " of the war.   Blenheim, Ramillies, Oudenarde and Malplaquet have made more noise in the world. But the controlling force in the whole war had been our dominance and the pervading influence of our mastery of communications at sea.   By this means we carried on our industries and commerce unchecked.   By the one we gained riches at home, supporting the demands of the war, and by the other we won wealth and power from other lands, which enabled us to establish our credit on an unassailable basis and to elevate the spirit of our people, thus, as Macaulay says of the war, laying " the deep and solid foundations on which was to rise the most gigantic fabric of commercial prosperity which the world has ever seen."   Naval supremacy is rooted in commercial prosperity, and without the one the other cannot be maintained.

The peace of the seas which we had won, enabled

us to develop the enormous resources of our growing Empire, and gave us means whereby to create the commercial supremacy which was to enable us to support the burden of the great wars that were to come before the century closed. Walpole was a peace minister. His object was to withhold the country from the continental engagements which threatened to entangle it, and he was enabled for about a quarter of a century to pursue this policy solely because the Navy was supreme at sea. " Madam," he said to Queen Caroline one morning in 1734, " there are fifty thousand men slain this year in Europe, and not one Englishman." It was naval supremacy alone that enabled a peaceful alliance with France to be established in 1717, and brought about the historic Quadruple Alliance of the following year.

We may pass over a considerable period of un-eventful character with a few observations, while we recognize the great significance of the time. One remarkable feature was a rapid revival of the Spanish Navy, under the powerful inspiration of Alberoni, but that new force had not ripened to the experi-ence of our own. It was helpless, and was utterly destroyed by Admiral George Byng, afterwards Viscount Torrington, in the action off Cape Passaro, on the 11th of August, 1718. Byng's secretary wrote of the action that the English might be said rather

" to have made a seizure than to have gotten a victory."

Peace was maintained only by power, and English naval power was used to impose peace upon Russia in her struggle with Sweden in the Baltic, whence we obtained naval stores, and where the balance was being changed to our disadvantage. We must observe also that peace was contributing rapidly to the commercial and maritime prosperity of France and French commerce—and with it the development of naval means—in Louisiana, Guadeloupe and Martinique, in the Mediterranean and Levant trade, and in India and the East, where Pondicherry, Chandernagore, the Ile Bourbon and the Ile de France were outposts of enterprise and power, and where a vast movement was inspired and directed by those great statesmen and administrators Dupleix and La Bourdonnais—the latter a seaman possessing a true instinct for sea power.

But, for the time being, France and England were the great barrier against war, and for many years were united in hostility to Spain. The fleet maintained control in the Baltic, it protected Gibraltar from a Spanish attack, and a detachment under command of Admiral Hozier was sent to Porto Bello, where it overawed the Spaniards, though the ships were ravaged with pestilence, and Hozier himself died (1726). Relations with

Spain were indeed becoming acute. Walpole might
strive for peace, but war was bound to come, and
it was declared in October, 1739. British commerce
had been subjected to impositions, searches and
stoppages in the Spanish possessions, and inhuman
cruelty was alleged by the West India merchants
to have been used towards the crews of English
ships. The case of "Jenkins's Ear"—Jenkins
was the master of a trading brig—the ear that was
torn off, had created a prodigious sensation in this
country, and Walpole had been overborne. Spain
held Florida, Mexico and the countries to the south,
and Cuba, Porto Rico and part of Hayti, and we
held Jamaica, Barbadoes and other islands, besides
the thirteen American colonies extending from
Maine to Georgia. Admiral Vernon made an attack
upon the Spanish Central American possessions,
falling suddenly upon Porto Bello (Nov. 21st; 1739),
but he found little treasure at that port, whence the
silver galleons were accustomed to sail. He was
reinforced by ships under Sir Challoner Ogle, and
joined by 12,000 troops which came under the
command of Wentworth, but the attacks on
Cartagena and Santiago de Cuba were unsuccessful.
Smollett, who was surgeon's mate in one of the ships,
has given in *Roderick Random* a caustic account of
the events at Cartagena, where, as at Santiago, the
want of success was due to military failure.

Want of co-operation between naval and military forces had led to Rooke's failure at Cadiz in 1702. "We are here," Colonel Stanhope had written, "not only divided sea against land, but land against land and sea against sea." There had been bitter jealousies during Peterborough's operations in Catalonia in 1706. Of the situation at Cartagena in 1701, Vernon wrote that he hoped to have orders to come home "being heartily sick of conjunct expeditions with the Army." Later on it was want of understanding between the naval and military forces, represented by John Byng and General Blakeney, that led to the loss of Minorca and the execution of Byng. These failures might be exemplified by other instances, and deserve attention, because they have diminished the proper influence and effect of sea power.

There was evidence also of a slow moral weakening within the Navy itself. There had grown up a spirit of professional self-satisfaction, whence had come no stimulus to efficiency, and no disposition to welcome criticism from without. Hence had arisen a tendency to unreality and formalism. The long peace did not spur the Navy to progress or change. Political embitterments affected it adversely, and the limited use of the fleet had caused its importance not to be realized. We were subsidizing foreign soldiers to fight for causes that were only in part our own, and money and interest were diverted from the naval service. The breath of life and the inspiration of commanding minds was wanting, and no standard existed of conduct nor a prevailing spirit of honour to direct all men alike. Some captains, like Hervey of the *Superb* in 1740, were brutal, others were self-seekers, and a few were men to whom patriotic loyalty to their chiefs and to the nation's interests made no appeal. There was corruption in administration, and the conditions of pay resulted in fraud upon the men, and bad and insufficient food, and harsh treatment filled the cup of their misery.

Our ships were inferior to those of the French, as was proved in the war. In 1719 the Navy Board laid down a scale of dimensions which proved a bar to progress, compelling shipwrights to observe formal rules, while the French and Spaniards were making many advances. Admiral Knowles wrote to the Admiralty in 1745 that our 70-gun ships were little superior to the French ships of 52 guns, and there were bitter complaints that our ships were crank, so that in blowing weather the lower-deck gun ports could not be opened. The ships were also weak in their scantling, which was a serious defect in winter weather, and they were too light in broadside fire. Fleets, moreover, were used in a manner that contributed to ineffective action. To discuss tactics

is impossible here, but the vigorous attack favoured
by Monk, De Ruyter and Tourville was out of favour,
and caution had taken its place.   There was no concentration on any part of the line, and as far as
possible ship was opposed to ship from van to rear.
We ought not, however, to conclude that this rigid
system was always due to a reluctance to push things
to a finish.   It sometimes arose from a reluctance
to accept risks.   There was great fear that the end
of the line might be doubled on, and to forestall this
action the practice was to bear down rapidly together
in order to bring the whole fleet into action as soon
as possible.

The conditions which have been suggested bore
evil fruit in some of the events that followed.   By
1743 the international weathercock had veered
round.   The War of the Austrian Succession had
broken out.   Spain had entered the continental
war and France was unofficially aiding her against
the Austrians in Italy.   Before Fleury, the friend
of England, died, a treaty was signed between the
two countries for joint operations, but war between
them had not been declared when Mathews met
the allies off Toulon in February, 1744.   Mathews
is described as " Il Furibondo " in Horace Mann's
correspondence with Walpole, but he was a good,
though not a brilliant officer, and no coward.
Lestock, his rear-admiral, has been pictured in

unfavourable colours by historians. He was un-
conciliatory, austere in command, restless as a
subordinate, with few friends. Campbell says he
was "an artful, vindictive disciplinarian," and
Beatson asserts that he and Mathews "bore each
other a most rancorous hatred." Thus the conditions were not favourable to success, and it is
worth while to note also that Mathews's age was
sixty-seven, and that of Lestock not much less,
while Nelson was only forty at the Nile and forty-
seven at Trafalgar.

The allied French and Spanish squadrons left
Toulon, with twenty-seven sail, on February 19th,
and Mathews, with twenty-nine ships, came up with
them three days later, but Lestock was several
miles to windward and to the rear. He made all
sail to join, but did not enter effectively into the
action. The Sailing Instructions had given sanc-
tion to his aloofness, and the Fighting Instructions
permitted him to make no use of his ships in
support of the Admiral. The signal for the line of
battle was flying when the signal to engage was
made, and he could not obey the latter without dis-
obeying the former! In the van, in the *Berwick*,
was Captain Edward Hawke—"the precursor of
Nelson"—who compelled the Spanish ship *Poder*
to strike. In the centre, where some captains were
shaken by Lestock's inaction, were several gallant

captains, and amongst them Edward Cornwall in the *Marlborough*, who fell fighting with 22 of his men. The allies were roughly handled, but the action did not place either the discipline or the intelligence of the Navy in a favourable light, and Mathews relinquished the pursuit. The "canker of a long peace" had ravaged it. The business ended in a series of courts martial, in which Mathews was condemned to be cashiered, because he had not pursued the allies, while Lestock, who had correctly observed regulations, was "honourably acquitted." As to the captains, several of them were awarded sentences according to their deserts.

There were other incidents at the time which showed the state into which the Fleet had fallen. Happily this was the dark shadow that preceded the dawn. The *Northumberland*, 74, was lost through the unofficerlike conduct of her captain, Watson, who was killed May 8th in 1744. Captain Elton of the *Anglesea*, 44, suffered the same fate on April 22nd in the next year, after rashly and disastrously engaging a French privateer, to which his ship struck. Confidence was lost. When Sir Charles Hardy left the French at sea under De Rochambeau in 1744, the Admiralty brought out from his retirement Sir John Balchen, at the age of seventy-five, a veteran of King William's wars, who drove the French to port, and, as he returned, perished with his flagship, the

Victory and over a thousand men, in a great storm in the Channel, on October 20th.

CHAPTER XI

ANSON AND HAWKE. THE REGENERATED NAVY

THE decline which was noted in the last chapter as preceding the dawn, forms a strange feature of naval history, though one not inscrutable, and it does not stand alone, for we shall find the same disastrous influences operating later on. But before the close of the War of the Austrian Succession in 1748, a new leaven was at work, which was beginning to lift the Navy to a height then unparalleled, though it could not save it from the colossal failure associated with the name of Byng. Anson and Hawke were the men of the new mould— Anson the great teacher, organizer and administrator, and Hawke, whom Admiral Mahan has aptly described as the " spirit " of the regenerated Navy.

Anson had shown great vigour in dealings with pirates on the coast of South Carolina and in other matters, and, when a commodore was required to proceed against the Spanish shipping on the West American coast, he was selected as one of the foremost seamen of the time. It has been said of him that he was " unchangeable of purpose, crafty of counsel, in triumph most sober, in failures of endurance beyond mortal man." In his memorable circumnavigation he had with him a band of men who were fit to be comrades of a hero, men who had no kinship with the Mathews, Lestocks and others of their kind. With his flag in the *Centurion*, 60, he had in his company the *Gloucester*, 50, *Severn*, 50, and three smaller vessels, and set sail on the 18th of September, 1740, short of seamen, and having 500 Chelsea pensioners in his ships, instead of the young soldiers who were to have formed part of his company. Scurvy broke out, and bad weather, bad food and insufficient clothing, with the effect of pestilential climates, afflicted his squadron grievously. The ships separated in the storms, some passing through Le Maire Strait and some round Cape Horn, and when the *Centurion* reached Juan Fernandez she had only 200 men alive out of 400, and most of them were incapacitated by disease and debility. The squadron was too weak to do anything against Panama, and Anson, having refitted his ships, encouraged his officers and men, and determined to cross the Pacific. There he intercepted the great Acapulco galleon on her way to Manila. This vessel, being carried to Macao for sale, proved to be worth more than £300,000, and was the richest prize of the time.

After a long and adventurous cruise, the *Centurion* reached Spithead on June 15th, 1744, and Anson, promoted to be rear-admiral of the white, went to the Admiralty before the close of that year. Then and later he wrought a profound change in administrative methods. The ships which were built under his impulsion were not the crank and lean-bowed craft of his recent experience, but were improvements upon French models, and the famous British "seventy-four" became the established type. Anson's ships had been a school of seamanship, several of his comrades rose to distinction, and many of them rendered valuable service to the State. His influence was felt throughout the naval organism, and it will be always his glory that he selected for high appointments officers like Hawke, Boscawen, Saunders, Rodney, Howe, and Keppel, and forged the weapons which most of them were to wield. He was relentless and remorseless in his efforts towards higher character and true discipline, and keen resentment was inevitably raised by the freedom with which he subjected unfit officers to what was sarcastically described as being " yellowed," that is appointed to an imaginary " yellow squadron."

Anson had no opportunities of gaining fame in great engagements, but when, as a vice-admiral, he met De la Jonquière off Cape Finisterre on the 3rd May, 1747, he wrought an important success in masterly fashion. The capture of Louisbourg in Cape Breton by a Colonial expedition convoyed by Commodore Warren in 1746, and danger in India, had stung the French into great efforts, and De la Jonquière was to carry a strong force to America, and detach Captain de Saint Georges, also with a strong force, to India. Both squadrons sailed together, fourteen vessels in all, including Indiamen, with transports and merchant vessels, and they were to separate at sea. Anson, with sixteen vessels, was to intercept the squadrons, and by skilful handling he brought them to action just as they were parting company. He was in great superiority, for only nine of the Frenchmen were fit to " lie in a line " against him. Anson formed no line of battle, but ordered a general chase. The French fought most gallantly, and inflicted serious loss upon us in officers and men, but the victory was complete, six sail of the line and four of the French India Company's ships being taken, though many of the merchantmen escaped. Thus a single action in European waters near home prevented reinforcements reaching two distant quarters of the world—an example of the all pervading influence of sea power.

The French, indeed, were unable to protect their commerce at sea, and serious economic results followed. Captain Thomas Fox, in June, 1747, commanding a small squadron, scattered the French convoy from San Domingo, and captured forty-eight prizes. The war had become world wide, and from 1744 onward small squadrons were sent to India, where the contest for power and commerce was increasing. Very little was accomplished there to our satisfaction, and even when Boscawen went out—one of the new race of officers—with the most powerful squadron ever seen in those waters, ten sail of the line and five smaller vessels, he could do little, because the soldiers failed him in the siege of Pondicherry and he himself had no experience as a general ashore.

The last important event of the war was Hawke's brilliant action with De l'Etenduère, on the 14th of October, 1747. A convoy of 250 merchantmen for the West Indies was about to leave Rochelle, and was to reach the destination after the hurricane season. The French admiral had his flag in the *Tonnant*, a splendid vessel of 80 guns, superior to anything we had yet built, and with him, to protect the large convoy, were seven other ships of the line, and a 64-gun East Indiaman. Hawke, whose conduct had shone brilliantly against the spiritless background of Mathews's action, was now a rear-admiral and had fourteen ships with him, all inferior in individual strength to the Frenchmen.

The admiral repeated the success of Anson
in the same way. When the strength of
L'Etenduère's squadron had been made out, a
general chase was ordered, and there followed a
desperate conflict, in which Hawke's ships were
much injured. The French admiral defended his
convoy nobly and successfully, and his captains
fought with great gallantry. L'Etenduère was
outnumbered, and six of his eight ships were
captured, much wrecked by our fire, but the
Tonnant was too powerful to be overcome, and broke
away with the *Intrépide*. The *Nottingham*, Captain
Philip Saumarez, and the ships of Captains Rodney
and Saunders, both to become famous admirals,
pursued, and Saumarez was killed. The French
merchantmen escaped, but without convoy, and
many of them were captured by our cruisers on
approaching their destination, for Hawke had
despatched a swift sloop to give tidings of their
coming.

Hawke has been styled the "precursor of
Nelson," and between these two great officers
there was certainly some kinship of temperament.
Nelson was possessed with a singleness of purpose
in pursuing his country's good that made him
regardless of self, and careless of prize money,
which was the reward of the service of many. The
same characteristics are found in Hawke who

might have detached some of his ships to deal with the convoy, but preferred to keep his squadron together for the purpose of defeating the striking force of the enemy. "I have nothing so much at heart as the faithful discharge of my duty ; this shall ever be my utmost ambition, and no lucre of profit or other views, shall induce me to act otherwise." "As to myself it is a matter of indifference to me whether, if I fight the enemy, they should come out, with an equal number, one ship more or one ship less." "If they can by any means be destroyed, it shall be done." "For God's sake, if you should be so lucky as to get sight of the enemy, get as close to them as possible." These sayings of Hawke's might have been said by Nelson, and they illustrate the character of the great seaman, whose commanding powers as a sea officer were yet to be shown in the glorious action of Quiberon Bay.

Both nations had suffered disastrous losses to their commerce, but the advantage, to the extent of £2,000,000, rested with England. We had entered upon the war badly, for the Navy had fallen from its high estate, and if an enemy had had a powerful fleet at sea, it would have gone very ill with us. But, before the war closed, Anson, Hawke and others, had added lustre to our naval annals. Lapeyrouse-Bonfils, the French naval historian, states that after the disaster to L'Etenduère, the

French flag disappeared from the sea. Privateers made a few prizes, and they almost always fell into English hands. British naval forces passed the sea without rivals. " And yet this sea power, which might have seized French and Spanish colonies, made few conquests from want of unity and per- sistence in the directions given."

The inconclusive Peace of Aix-la-Chapelle (April, 1748), left many questions unsettled, and gave the promise of future trouble. Practically it left the situation unchanged. France and England relinquished the conquests they had made during the war, and France abandoned the cause of the Stuarts. Such a conclusion was perhaps inevitable after the inconclusive character of the naval struggle. There had been military defeat abroad, a Stuart had landed on the coast of Scotland, and the hopes of the Jacobites ran high. Exhaustion had fallen upon the nations, and they hastened to make peace. In effect it was only a truce. Were the fortunes of the New World to be moulded by Englishmen or Frenchmen ? Was India to be attached to the dominions of England or France ? These were the questions which the coming war was to settle, thus shaping the destiny of mankind.

CHAPTER XII

THE SEVEN YEARS' WAR AND WORLD DOMINION

THE Seven Years' War, dating from 1756, began actually in the previous year. There had been no real peace, for no ferment had perturbed the world by which we had not been stirred. The Channel, the Ocean, the Mediterranean, India, the North American coast, and the West Indies, all these regions were, or became, the scenes of strife. Inevitably we cannot here describe a world-wide conflict. Our purpose must be rather to indicate the general direction and character of the war, to touch upon some salient features, and to arrive at an understanding of certain lessons.

Men of progressive mind, of the mould of Anson and Hawke, did not view the approach of war with misgiving. They were in conflict with enormous difficulties at home, in their work, and there were some things in the camp of the enemy which they, or some of them, did not know or fully realize. It was not a system originated in peace that was to be tested by the war. In the school of fighting the reform of the fighting service began. In the lessons of the fighting the need of better discipline had been discerned. There must be no more failures like

that of Mathews and Lestock. Thenceforth, under
the revised Articles of War, he who, through cowardice, negligence or disaffection, failed to "relieve or
assist a known friend in view to the utmost of his
power" was adjudged, without alternative, to have
merited the penalty of death. The uniform first
established for officers in 1748 was not to be dis-
honoured, and the ferocity that was displayed
in the treatment of Byng was the grim measure of
the astonishment and indignation of the Government
and the service at this new instance of incapacity.
Anson's work had included the giving of a new
impulse to naval architecture and construction,
and though the dockyards were still in a sad state
of disarray, they were better administered. The
manning of the Navy was the most serious difficulty,
and extraordinary efforts were made to procure
men by the press rigorously applied, by bounties,
and even by accepting gaol-birds, and practically
to hold the rabble in awe, the Marines—originating
in the Duke of York and Albany's Maritime Regiment
of Foot in 1666—were placed upon a permanent
footing in 1755 at the outbreak of the war.

The trouble began in North America in that
year. The French were expelling our colonists
from the valleys of the Ohio and Mississippi, and
Fort Duquesne built at the fork of the former river,
on the spot whence the colonists had been driven, was

the sign of their overthrow, made doubly despiteful by the disastrous failure of Braddock to recapture it. While our colonists were making their homes in the coast region, Champlain and his comrades had established settlements in Canada and Acadie, and La Salle had carried his vessels from the great lakes, by the Mississippi, to the Gulf of Mexico, where the French were secure in the possession of Louisiana. They were claiming all the country west of the Alleghenies, and that great governor Montcalm was laying his plans to cut off our colonists from access to the west. Thus it was that when the French sent out reinforcements under Dubois de Lamotte, Boscawen had orders to intercept them. He failed in his object, and captured on June 10th, 1755, only the *Alcide*, 64, and a smaller ship. This act, with the seizure of the *Espérance* and some trading vessels a little later, was denounced by the French as piracy. Lord Hardwicke told the Duke of Newcastle that we had done either too much or too little. If we had meant to strike at all, we ought to have struck hard.

Uncertain objects led to uncertain orders, and Hawke at sea with sixteen sail, did not succeed in preventing the return of De Lamotte to Brest, where a squadron was being fitted for operations. Hawke was recalled, and Admiral John Byng—*infelix nomen*—replaced him. Boscawen's squadron was

paralysed by disease on the other side of the
Atlantic. Hawke had failed, and the French were
once more planning an invasion, this time under
command of Marshal Belleisle. A shameful panic
thereupon demoralized the land. Every French
port was bustling with armaments, and Newcastle's
government, denounced by Pitt, was ready to import
both Dutch and Hessians to defend us. The sea-
ward vocation of the country was forgotten. " The
clamours of the merchants," wrote Horace Walpole,
" sometimes reasonable, always self-interested, ter-
rified the Duke of Newcastle, and, while, to prevent their outcries in the City of London, he minced
the navy of England into cruisers and convoys,
every other service was neglected." Newcastle's
fears did not infect Anson, but it is now impossible
properly to allocate responsibility for the distribution
of the fleet, though popular clamour seems to have
influenced it. Certain it is that the French were
not ready at Brest, that the invasion was an im-
possibility, and that too large a force was maintained
in the Channel, while the position at Minorca, where
General Blakeney was calling for reinforcements
was neglected.

The result of all this was that 15,000 French
troops under command of the Duc de Richelieu,
convoyed by that very able sea-officer the Marquis
de la Galissonière, landed in Minorca, where Mahon

was blockaded by sea and land when Byng arrived
with a squadron of thirteen sail. He well knew
that sooner or later the place would fall unless men
could be landed, and he had no men available.
Therefore he had no choice but to bring De la
Galissonière to action, which he did on the 20th May,
1756. The engagement has been much discussed.
It was inconclusive, and though the French lost
three ships, the main body escaped without serious
damage. There had been great bungling in the
handling of our ships, the naval fight had not been
fought to a finish, and then no help was extended
to the beleaguered citadel of Mahon. Instead, on
the advice of a council of war, that resource of
weak men, Byng left Minorca to its fate, and went
to Gibraltar lest an attack should be delivered there.

There followed a howl of indignation in England,
and a cry went up for a victim. Hawke had gone
out to replace Byng, who came home, and a court
martial on the 2nd February, 1757, found him
guilty of negligence, and condemned him to death—
the only punishment authorized under the new
Articles of War. Byng was shot on the quarter-deck
of the *Monarque* in Portsmouth harbour on the 14th of
March. It was not without a pang that the members
of the court had condemned a brother officer to death;
they would willingly have spared him the tragic
penalty of his failure ; but the service rebelled

against the type of leadership which the unfortunate admiral had exemplified.

It must be observed that events in Europe were
largely subsidiary or ancillary to the struggle for
dominion in the New World. Also that the
system of controlling an enemy by close blockade
had not at that time been perfected as it was later
by St Vincent. Intermittent watching not sufficing,
two several expeditions from Brest and Rochefort
and one from Toulon got to the westward, giving
the French commander-in-chief eighteen sail of the
line and five frigates. Pitt had succeeded Newcastle, and formed projects for the capture of
Louisbourg and Quebec, whereby French power in
North America might be destroyed. Accordingly
Boscawen, conveying Amherst with 13,000 troops,
in a hundred and fifty transports, sailed for Halifax,
and in July, 1758, Louisbourg was taken, the French
loss being four sail of the line burned and one captured.
Just a year later Vice-Admiral Saunders and General
Wolfe—one of the happiest illustrations of complete
understanding between the two services in all our
annals—left Spithead, and on the 17th February,
1759, Quebec fell before the dying hero in an action
which is glorious in all our military story, though
the essential service of the Fleet is too often over-
looked by the historian. The mastery of the
seaman's art which Saunders displayed at that time,

a combination of daring caution, skill and command, has rarely been surpassed.

The year 1759 was the *annus mirabilis* of the century. It was the year in which the younger Pitt was born, and that witnessed not only the fall of Quebec, but the victory of Minden, the capture of Guadeloupe and Goree, and the third inconclusive action between Pocock and D'Aché on the coast of Coromandel, which, combined with the naval exhaustion of France, caused her to abandon the East India Seas, and inevitably led to the fall of French power in India. Still more, it witnessed the sea victories of Boscawen and Hawke, whereby England once again was saved. Thus we have reached a " seamark " in our imperial history. North America and India were slipping from the hand of France, and the heart of the empire was secure. But all this was not understood at the time. The French plan was that Vice-Admiral de Conflans should command the main fleet at Brest, that De la Clue should join him from Toulon, and that Thurot, a brave privateer with a squadron at Dunkirk, should make a diversion against the coasts of Scotland and Ireland. There came a time when Thurot escaped to the Baltic and had to be watched there, when Hawke was driven by storms off his blockading station at Ushant, and when Conflans put to sea. Panic stalked once more through the land, and Hawke was burned in effigy even on the very day when he won imperishable fame. But the first blow was struck on the 18th of August by Boscawen, in a very fine action, equally gallant on both sides, in which De la Clue was defeated, and all hope of his joining Conflans came to an end.

A large body of troops for the intended invasion under command of D'Aiguillon had been mustered around Quiberon Bay, where transports were ready, and Conflans was to issue from Brest, and escort them to the intended place of disembarkation. Hawke had been driven to Torbay by a great gale, and the French admiral put to sea on November 14th. The wind that favoured him also enabled Hawke to get away from Torbay. Captain Duff, with a small squadron, had been watching the transports in Quiberon Bay, and only just escaped on the appearance of Conflans, who had decided to remain in the Bay, with the transports, until another gale should blow Hawke from his station. He did not know what manner of man Hawke was, nor foresee the character of the attack.

Quiberon Bay lies about 150 miles south-east from Ushant, protected from the west and south-west by the Quiberon peninsula, Belle Isle, and the rugged Cardinal rocks, with other dangerous rocks and shoals, well known to the French, but little to Englishmen in Hawke's time. It was on the 20th of November, with a gale from the westward blowing, that Hawke sighted Conflans in his flagship, the *Soleil Royal*, rounding the Cardinals. Darkness was approaching, when Hawke in the *Royal George*, 100 guns, "came swooping from the west," and Conflans did not suppose that his adversary would venture his fleet in those perilous and uncharted waters, and attack at headlong speed, in a heavy sea, with the wind driving him towards a lee shore. But Hawke knew his ships and men, and what risks he could run. His own sailing-master remonstrated, but the Admiral was not to be held back. "You have done your duty, Sir," he said, "in showing the danger; you have now to comply with my order and lay me alongside the *Soleil Royal*." Thus was the battle gained, one of the most desperate ever fought by a British fleet. The French ships were scattered, many of them shattered by gun-fire, some captured, others driven on shoals, and two sunk. Conflans' flagship went ashore and was burned, with another. Several other ships ran up the bay, threw their guns overboard, and escaped into the Vilaine river, where they remained for many months. Hawke lost two ships on the rocks, but his victory was glorious and decisive, and, night having fallen, he anchored the fleet, "being on a part of the coast among islands and shoals of which we were totally ignorant, without a pilot, as was the greatest part of the squadron, and

blowing hard on a lee shore." Hawke's name will
ever be immortalized by his magnificent victory over
men, the stormy seas and the perilous rocks off
Quiberon, whereby invasion was averted once more.
The victory was the Trafalgar of the time, without
precedent and without a successor for forty years to
come.

The Peace of Paris, November, 1762, did not
content the country, but it marked our triumph.
In North America, by cession from France and
Spain, we obtained an empire embracing Canada
and all the present United States east of the Mississippi. We retained Tobago, Dominica, St Vincent,
and Grenada, in the West Indies ; and in India
the French military establishment was given up.
Louisiana passed to Spain.

CHAPTER XIII

THE WAR OF AMERICAN INDEPENDENCE

IT has been said of the Seven Years' War that
while it continued the trade of England increased
every year, and that such national prosperity,
during a long, costly and bloody war had never
before been shown by any people in the world. The
French Navy had been practically annihilated, and
the main objection to the peace was that it left to

France opportunities of building up her fleet anew. They were opportunities of which she made good use. The great work of the Duc de Choiseul, which ended in 1770, to be taken up later by M. de Sartine and that able minister Turgot, was in effect to revive and regenerate the Navy, in numbers, organization and discipline, and to foster the alliance with Spain. In England many causes led to a certain pause in preparation for war, for which also there existed an evident distaste, as when Corsica was given over to France, being an alienation which the veteran Admiral Sir Charles Saunders would have made a *casus belli*. The trouble with the American colonies began with the Stamp Act of 1765, and was coming to a head when Louis XV died in 1774. The great French plan was to take advantage of our difficulties, and again to threaten the heart of the empire, so that power of resistance at its extremities might be diminished.

Within the British service the war had borne great fruit, and everything that conduced to fighting efficiency was upon a better footing than before, including the health of the seamen. All this was shown in the infinitely better state of the squadrons of Rodney and Hood, as, later, of St Vincent and Nelson. The example of Captain Cook in fighting scurvy and fever, and the work of Sir Gilbert Blane, physician to the fleet in Rodney's time, and of others, effected a wonderful change for the better. This was the work of seamen, but under the rule of Lord Sandwich, from 1771 onward, administration decayed. Political corruption and jobbery again worked their evil end, and money was voted which was never applied to the purpose intended. Thus, while in many respects the Navy was in a better posture for fighting, there were serious defects, and this at a time when, in 1778, it was to be matched with the regenerated Navy of France, allied in 1779 with a respectable Spanish force, and in 1780 with the small but efficient navy of the Dutch. Already the admirals on the American station, where Howe assumed command in July, 1776, had not been given force sufficient to deal with the situation. American privateers were ravaging commerce and cutting off or menacing supplies, with the practical countenance of France and Spain. In short we were about to be presented with a situation analogous to that of Spain in former times, with her great disjointed empire, in a war which extended throughout the world.

The surrender of Burgoyne at Saratoga, on the 17th of October, 1777, was the spark that kindled the flame, and in February, 1778, the French recognised the independence of the United States, and in March the war began. As with the last war, so here we can deal only with certain points of the conflict. The seizure of Pondicherry, and the arrival of Sir Edward Hughes with eight sail of the line, followed three years later by that great French officer Suffren, marked the new conflict for dominance in India. In home waters the situation was unfavourable, and when Keppel encountered the French, under D'Orvilliers off Ushant, in equal strength, on the 27th of July, an inconclusive action followed in which neither fleet suffered much damage. This effete performance was followed by a very acrimonious wrangle between Keppel and Sir Hugh Palliser, who was accused of having prevented his chief from gaining a victory, and Sandwich encouraged and permitted Palliser to bring Keppel before a court martial. This fact is mentioned in order to show how politics were influencing and undermining discipline, as they too often do.

Meantime D'Estaing, with twelve sail of the line and four frigates, had crossed the Atlantic, and appeared off Sandy Hook on the 12th of July, finding Howe at a great disadvantage. But, characteristically, as a French officer, he withdrew rather than run great risks, though the stroke might have justified bold enterprise. Howe had pursued a masterly defensive, and the French officer, on his part, showed no disposition to attack, so that the naval events of the summer were inconclusive. Howe was relieved by Byron and came home, with his brother the general, resentful at the want of support that had been given to him during the trouble with the colonists. " He had been deceived into his command, and he was deceived while he retained it." Political factions and personal jealousies were undermining the spirit of the Navy, and there was a saying that " if a naval officer were to be roasted, another officer could always be found to turn the spit." Sandwich's profligate rule had disgusted and in some ways demoralized the service. Howe was, he said, unwilling " to trust the little reputation he had earned by forty years' service, his personal honour and everything else he held dear, in the hands of men who had neither the ability to act on their own judgment, nor the integrity and good sense to follow the advice of others, who might know more of the matter." So completely was the Navy sacrificed to party that Barrington, a very distinguished officer, refused to take command of a fleet. " Who," he wrote, " would trust himself in chief command with such a set of scoundrels as are now in office ? " These facts show that there existed a very serious weakness in the service at a critical time.

Howe was succeeded by Byron—known as " Foul Weather Jack " from his ceaseless conflicts with the elements—and there was much inconclusive manœuvring, with the capture of islands in the West Indies. It must not be supposed that the reluctance of D'Estaing and other French admirals to engage

an enemy in the manner of Hawke, Howe and
Nelson, was due to cowardice. Their object was to
keep their fleets in being for some ulterior purpose,
such as attacking their enemy's possessions, exhausting his resources, or weakening his commercial
and maritime power. Rodney, whose name was to
be raised to high fame in these waters, fresh from his
relief of Gibraltar, arrived on the West Indies station
at Santa Lucia on the 27th of March, 1780, and on the
17th of April to leeward—that is west, for the east is
the persistent breeze—of Dominica, having 20 sail,
met De Guichen, a brave and accomplished officer,
who had succeeded D'Estaing, and had 22 ships
with his flag. The French officer soon saw that his
opponent meant no formal parade, but a determined
attack with his whole force on the French rear. He
warded off the danger by turning his fleet, and both
fleets went north. Again the same opportunity
came to Rodney, but Captain Carkett, commanding
the leading ship, a bulldog seaman, failed to under-
stand, and, acting in the spirit of the old school,
made sail, followed by other ships, with the intention
of reaching De Guichen's van. Thus the action
became ineffective, and Rodney bitterly accused
his subordinates of deliberately wrecking the battle.
Carkett was unintelligent, but Rodney was reserved,
and appears never to have explained his intentions
to his captains, as Nelson did to his "band of

brothers." After this action Rodney put his fleet through a series of strenuous manœuvres, and twice came again into touch with De Guichen, who, having the wind of him, declined to be brought to action, and the operations remained inconclusive.

The pressure of the situation was now telling heavily upon our naval resources. The capture, by a French and Spanish force, of 63 sail of Indiamen, transports and merchantmen, intended for the West Indies, showed how commerce was menaced. When the Dutch ranged themselves against us, the trade in the North Sea had to be protected, and a squadron of old vessels under command of Sir Hyde Parker— " Vinegar Parker "—-was engaged in the duties, and had a sanguinary but inconclusive battle at the Dogger Bank (5th August, 1781) with the Dutch under Zoutman, each fleet fighting ship to ship in the·old style.

But the real scene of interest was across the Atlantic, where the French were using their fleets so intelligently that ultimately the independence of the United States was established. Yet things might have gone otherwise. The Comte de Grasse was sent out from Brest with a great armament. There was no blockade to prevent his issuing from the port. So urgent and insistent were the demands on the Navy that home waters were deprived of an adequate force of ships of the line. There can be little doubt that we lay under the shadow of disaster. When Admiral Darby with a powerful force was in the vicinity of De Grasse off the south coast of Ireland, he did not strive to bring him to action. He had other objects in view. Yet if De Grasse had been destroyed there and then, the history of North America might have been differently written. On the other hand if De Grasse had annihilated Darby, Gibraltar would not have been relieved, a squadron and Indiamen for the Cape of Good Hope might have been cut off, and a reinforcement of ships and men might not have reached the West Indies.

It was not easy for Sandwich to find a successor to " Vinegar Parker," who had been Rodney's second in command. They had not agreed, and when Parker had returned it was in high dudgeon. Samuel Hood was chosen, one of our ablest sea officers, whom Rodney knew well, but a stern critic who had little of admiration for his chief, or for some other officers of the time. He thought Graves cunning and incompetent, though posterity does more justice to that officer. To Hood, Rowley was silly, Pigot a nonentity, and Douglas feeble to the verge of imbecility. But as time went on Hood's chief contempt was for his own chief, who, it must be confessed, being a man much embarrassed by want of money, interested himself vastly in the huge booty at Saint Eustatius, which the Dutch declaration of war had placed at his mercy, but of which a large part was captured by the French under La Motte Picquet on its way home.

The arrival of De Grasse did not bring the results the French had looked for. He declined to be entangled in an engagement with Hood on the 1st of May, 1781, and, as was customary, damaged the English ships in masts and spars, reducing some of them to temporary impotence. Later on he eluded and baffled Rodney also. Graves, reinforced by Hood, failed against the French at the Chesapeake, and Cornwallis surrendered with his army at Yorktown. Thus the independence of the United States was won.

But the Navy could yet deal hard blows at the enemy. While Hood was outmatched in the West Indies, Kempenfelt, 150 miles west of Ushant, practically annihilated a force which was to have joined De Grasse. Kempenfelt is best known to posterity because he was lost, with 800 souls, by the capsizing of his old and rotten flagship, the *Royal George*, at Spithead on the 29th of August, 1782.

> "His sword was in its sheath,
>   His fingers held the pen,
> When Kempenfelt went down,
>   With twice four hundred men."

It was well that he should die so, for the veteran

officer exercised with his pen a potent influence upon
the Navy, his insight and inspiration being a great
force in elevating its character and reforming its
tactics.

Rodney, in ill-health, had come home, but was
out with a fine squadron early in 1782. The French
squadron, to be joined by the Spaniards from Cuba,
and with troops from Martinique, was to fall upon
Jamaica, and the opportunity Rodney desired was
given into his hand. The French admiral was
hampered by his convoy of 150 sail, and had to
detach ships for its protection, so that on the great day
he had only 33 sail of the line with his flag, while
Rodney had 36 highly efficient and powerfully armed
ships. The light and unstable airs prolonged the
action. On the 8th of April De Grasse got to sea, and
on the 9th, recognizing his danger, he sent his convoy
into Guadeloupe, and was brought to action by the
necessity of saving two of his ships which had fallen
to leeward. He might have fallen upon the van
under Hood with superior force, but, with his ulterior
object in mind, he was content with a cannonade.
The great action took place on the 12th, and the
glory of the day was the crown of Rodney's career.
We cannot describe the breaking of the line, which
illuminated the new tactics of the fleet. The *Ville
de Paris*, flagship of De Grasse, with the admiral
on board, struck to the *Barfleur*, flying the flag of

Sir Samuel Hood, and four other ships of the line
were taken. Much more might have been done.
Hood told Rodney that twenty ships might have been
captured, and would himself have liked to take up
the chase. " Come, we have done very handsomely
as it is," said Rodney. There was nothing in him
of Nelson's fiery resolve to destroy the enemy where-
ever he could be found. Sir Charles Douglas,
captain of the fleet, and Cornwallis and other captains
all deplored the failure to reap the full fruit of the
victory. Nelson afterwards expressed the same
view.

We conclude this record of the War of American
Independence with a reference to Howe's magnificent
relief of Gibraltar, long besieged, in 1782, and to
the five actions which Suffren fought with Hughes
in Indian waters. In none of them did he take an
English ship, nor did he succeed in his main object,
but Frenchmen dwell with legitimate pride upon
his achievements, and we cannot but recognize that
Suffren was a really great man and a fine seaman,
who inspired his fleet, and brought it within an ace
of victory.

We had been confronted in the war by the triple
alliance of France, Spain and Holland, at a time
when these powers were not embroiled in any continental complications, and we were at the same time
trying to subjugate our rebellious colonists. The

French Navy was in a highly efficient state, while our Navy had suffered relative decline. The corruption of the House of Commons, the virulent bitterness of partizans, dissension in the Cabinet and faction in the country, combined with the corrupt administration of Sandwich, had undermined. the spirit of the service. We were outmatched in numbers, and unable to defend what we had won. But, though we lost the American Colonies, we consolidated elsewhere our dominions, and the Navy emerged the better from the struggle, which ended in.1783, and already on the pathway to the period of its greatest splendour.

CHAPTER XIV

THE FRENCH REVOLUTION. HOWE. PROJECTS
OF INVASION AND THE MUTINIES

PITT, being a Peace Minister, strove hard to withstand the tempest that was driving us rapidly towards war with Revolutionary France, but was swept into the vortex when the Revolutionary army invaded Holland, and the declaration of hostilities was delivered in February, 1793. The army establishments had been allowed to sink to the lowest degree of weakness and inefficiency, but fortunately the Navy continued upon the high level to which it had been raised. Throughout the long war its officers, with few exceptions, were men of high capacity and courage and not seldom of brilliant attainments, and though the fleet carried within itself, on the lower deck, seeds of disaffection which were to ripen into mutiny four years later, its officers were able to lead it and regenerate it, with the most advantageous results for the country and the world. For a number of years the miserable impotence of our efforts on land was, in effect, matched with an unbroken record of success at sea.

The French Navy had been greatly demoralized by the Revolution. The monarchy had left behind it the elements of a fine fleet in 75 ships with 6000 guns—we had 115 ships with about 8700 guns—but the dockyards were in a shocking state, and bitter rancour, and the memory of many hardships and wrongs filled the ships with discontent or mutiny. The old corps of officers had almost disappeared. Its members were either *émigrés* or had gone to the scaffold, and with them had gone the spirit of discipline. Their successors were men who generally received command because their *civisme* had been declared or tried, and they eagerly donned the republican *cocarde*. They were mostly drawn from the mercantile marine, the habits of the trader adhered to some of them, and many of them gained their first notions of naval tactics in the presence of the enemy. Some of these officers were rank cowards, and, even as late as the date of the Battle of the Nile, Trullet, commanding the *Timoléon*, said their poltroonery affected the men, and he had seen them escaping from their ships when they ought to have been fighting the enemy. In Humbert's ships, in the disastrous expedition to Ireland (1798), mutiny was rife, and when Bompard put to sea, his unpaid men were in revolt, and he had to cut his way through with his sword to see the ringleaders put in irons. Yet as we shall see, the fighting spirit was not dead. The French were, indeed, stimulated, and not cowed by reverses. The spirit of the sea eluded them, but on land they called a population to arms, set a million men in array, and produced perhaps the greatest military genius that the world has ever known. Thus it was that Austria, Prussia, Sardinia, Spain and Holland, which were at first leagued with us against the Revolution, fell away one after another from the alliance, until at last we stood alone.

The great difficulty in 1793 was the raising of men, which was effected by means of a very " hot press " in all the seaports. Every available seaman was caught in the naval net, and thereby a good deal of misery was caused, as also by the great rise in the cost of provisions, which reduced the pay to starvation level. Every vessel capable of service was made fit for her duties. The advantage of coppering the ships had been fully recognized at the beginning of the American War, and many went to sea which would otherwise have rotted in harbour. Three-decked ships were built in increasing numbers.

The strategy of the Admiralty and the Government provided for the exertion of our naval power chiefly in three regions of the world. In April and May, twenty sail, under command of Lord Hood, went to the Mediterranean. Before the close of the year Sir John Jervis, the future Earl St Vincent—great sea officer and stern disciplinarian—departed with four sail of the line, and 7000 troops under command of Sir C. Grey, to the West Indies where Martinique, Santa Lucia, and Guadeloupe were occupied, but the occupation was the work of soldiers, and the chequered events did not affect the results of the war.

In the Mediterranean, Hood, by agreement with the Royalists, occupied Toulon, and the new garrison also included Spaniards, Piedmontese and Neapolitans. No counter-revolution resulted, as had been expected, and the place being menaced by attack on the land side, it was evacuated amid terrible scenes, and Hood departed, carrying away some French ships and crowds of refugees. Other ships were destroyed, as well as the arsenal. At Toulon Napoleon Bonaparte, then a young artillery officer, for the first time set eyes upon the British fleet. As we all know, in the coming years, to use a classic phrase " those far distant, storm-beaten ships, upon which the Grand Army never looked, stood between it and the dominion of the world."

In the Channel and ocean, where Howe was to strike the first blow, the year 1793 was uneventful, for the French were as yet powerless, though, under command of Villaret-Joyeuse, extraordinary efforts were made to prepare the main fleet at Brest.   When it put to sea on the 16th May, 1794, it was in a better state than any French squadron we met during the remainder of the war.   Meantime Admiral Vanstabel had escaped from Brest, in the previous December, to cross the Atlantic, in order to convoy home a huge fleet of grain ships, and Admiral Nielly in April had also got away to meet him.   Howe did not maintain the close form of blockade which is associated with the name of St Vincent.   He had not the same means, and he did not desire to keep the French in Brest.   Like Nelson, he wished to meet them at sea.   He had orders to intercept the grain convoy, but like old British admirals, he knew that the thing that really mattered was to destroy the enemy's fighting fleet, and in effect Vanstabel's convoy escaped him.

The two fleets were in sight of one another on the 28th of May, and on that day and the next Howe made determined attacks on the French rear. On the 28th the huge *Révolutionnaire*, 110 guns, bore the brunt, and having damaged some of her assailants severely, made off to Brest. The following two days were occupied in manœuvring in light airs and fogs, and on the morning of " the Glorious First of June," the French were discovered ahead, on the lee bow, with twenty-six sail, being one ship more than Howe had with his flag. We shall not describe the battle, much discussed as it has been. More desirable it is to observe its salient features. It was an exemplification, in its highest form, of the new tactics of the fleet. Anson and Hawke, and Captain Cornwall, who was killed in Mathews's action of 1744, had planted the seed, Kempenfelt had worked, Clerk of Eldin (not a seaman) had written a book on the new tactics, and Rodney had broken the enemy's line on the 12th of April, 1782. But the inspiration had come from France—from the fleet we were to beat—from the teachings of Père Hoste, Bigot de Morogues, De Vilhuet, and Mahé de la Bourdonnais.

Howe revised the signals and removed the tactical fetters, and on the " Glorious First of June," made the action " close," by bearing down line to line with the object of breaking through at every part, cutting off retreat, and making the enemy fight the battle out to the end. He had the wind,

and passing through the line the ships were to
fight from " to leeward." " I don't want the ships
to be bilge to bilge," he said, " but if you can lock
the yard-arms so much the better ; the battle will
be the quicker decided." The order was not, and
perhaps could not have been obeyed in every part, but
the English ships were soon furiously engaged with
the Frenchmen. The most tragic incident was the
fight between the *Brunswick* and the *Vengeur*, which
was a desperate affair, Captain Harvey being mortally
wounded, and the *Vengeur*, after surrendering,
sinking with a great part of her company. We
captured six prizes, and if Howe had been a younger
man, might have captured more, but he was sixty-
eight, and worn out, though displaying an animation,
says an eye-witness, " of which, at his age, and after
such fatigue of body and mind, I should not have
thought him capable."

The effect of this splendid action, of other losses,
of Bridport's defeat of Villaret-Joyeuse on the 23rd
of June, 1795, and of the decay of the French fleet,
deprived it of power. The events described and others
in the Mediterranean then forced upon the French
mind the old idea, by evasion of the fleet, to strike a
blow at their enemy's heart, and projects of invasion
abounded. The ridiculous Fishguard "invasion,"
under the notorious Tate, with 1500 liberated
criminals, who forthwith surrendered, was an

absurdity and a comedy. The futile expedition of Hoche to Bantry Bay, engendered in strife, and dogged by misfortune, ended in perilous failure. Villaret-Joyeuse quarrelled with Hoche, and Morard de Galles was appointed, protesting that he possessed none of the qualities necessary and that he was old, ill and partially blind. "Another victory!" wrote the general, "he is the very man for the business; if his eyes are feeble we will see for him." But both Admiral and General escaped by a miracle from an English pursuing ship, and were not with their friends when they landed at Bantry—landed without a guinea, a tent, or a horse to drag their four useless guns. The Frenchmen who stole back to Brest were thankful that nothing worse had happened to them.

There was a subsequent project of landing 70,000 men in England, under the ægis of the French, Spanish and Dutch fleets—for our former allies were now against us—but Jervis's splendid triumph off Cape St Vincent, on the 14th of February, followed by Duncan's great and not sufficiently appreciated victory at Camperdown, on the 11th of October, 1797, put an end to the whole scheme. It was revived, however, against Ireland in 1798, where the rebellion seemed to promise results, but such was the pressure of the British fleet that the expedition had to be divided into six expeditions, of which five put to sea, two being utter failures and two disasters, while only one, that of Humbert, attained an impotent measure of success.

We see, therefore, once again the Navy shielding the Empire's heart, defeating its enemies at sea, and extending its sway, for this was the period in which we were enriched with the splendid acquisitions of the Cape of Good Hope, Ceylon and other places won from the enemy. The Mediterranean events shall be dealt with in the next chapter.

But there is another side to the picture. The seeds of disaffection which have been alluded to, were now breaking into the evil growth of mutiny, and the year 1797, which opened so brilliantly, became one of gloomy character for the country. Finance was in a desperate condition, and the Bank of England suspended its cash payments. In April the seamen at Spithead became openly rebellious, dismissed their officers, and hoisted the red flag. Their grievances were many and real, their demands were moderate and they maintained some of the forms of discipline. When their claims had been granted, with promise of an amnesty, the mutiny came to an end. It broke out, however, with more menacing and criminal features at the Nore, presenting the appearance of revolution, and causing the seamen at Spithead to declare that the conduct was a " scandal to the name of British seamen." If it had not been for good and capable officers, and

chiefs like Howe and St Vincent, the situation
might have proved very dangerous. But Duncan's
victory at Camperdown showed that the malady of
mutiny was not really deep, and that the Navy was
sound at heart after all.

CHAPTER XV

NELSON, THE MEDITERRANEAN AND THE NILE.
THE PEACE OF AMIENS

THE brilliant events in the Mediterranean, which
were made illustrious by the battle of the Nile,
were contemporary with some of the occurrences
that have been described.   There were two theatres
of operations in the same war, for Bonaparte, while
shaping his great Mediterranean policy, which involved the subjugation of the states of Italy, with
a splendid aspiration towards dominion in India,
was still seeking to weld into his combination
against us, the Spaniards, the Dutch and the
Northern Powers.   Here in the Mediterranean we
meet Nelson, captain of the *Agamemnon* in 1793, an
officer not much known at that time, nor particularly well liked, but destined to become the most
popular of captains and the greatest of admirals.
The profitless occupation of Corsica has obtained

its chief celebrity owing to the fact that Nelson contributed much to the success at Bastia and lost his right eye at Calvi. Hotham had succeeded Hood, and being an officer of the older type, he conducted his action of March, 1795, in such an inconclusive manner that the contempt of Nelson was evoked. Nelson believed that not only the *Ça Ira* and *Censeur*, which he had been chiefly instrumental in capturing, would have fallen to us, but that the whole French fleet would have been destroyed. Almost in the words of Rodney, after the engagement of the 12th of April, 1782, Hotham said to him, " We must be contented ; we have done very well " ; but Nelson wrote to his wife, " Now had we taken ten sail, and had allowed the eleventh to escape, when it had been possible to have got at her, I could never have called it well done."

The French were reinforced by six sail of the line, under command of Renaudin, the hero of the *Vengeur* on the Glorious First of June—a force which the Admiralty had allowed to slip round from Brest, to Nelson's surprise—and Admiral Man came out therefore with reinforcements. A second inconclusive action took place on July 13th, Hotham recalling his ships from the chase. Knowing what Nelson afterwards accomplished at the Nile, we may say with certainty that a decisive victory might have been attained, and then the history of the war would

8—2

have been written differently. The Riviera road would have been made impassable to the French army, the splendid actions of Bonaparte might never have been fought, the whole history of Italy would have been changed, and probably Spain would have kept aloof from the French alliance.

Jervis replaced Hotham, and immediately imparted new vigour to the squadron, but the Spaniards declared war on the 5th of October, 1796, Corsica became untenable and was abandoned, and Admiral Man, who was at Gibraltar, thinking an impossible task had been imposed upon him, in orders received from Jervis that he should proceed from Gibraltar to join the flag at Elba, came home instead, to the exasperation of the Admiral. Thus the abandonment of the Mediterranean became necessary, so unfortunate for us in its consequences, and " so dishonourable to the dignity of England," said Nelson, " whose fleets are equal to meet the world in arms," and thus, too, the battle of the 14th February, 1797, was fought off Cape St Vincent, instead of in the inland sea.

That famous St Valentine's Day battle has been many times described. Owing to a signal made by Jervis, directing a faulty tactical movement, it would not have proved decisive if Nelson had not disobeyed the order, and taken upon himself to wear out of the line, and stand down to meet the Spanish

admiral in the *Santisima Trinidad*, the largest
ship then afloat. Nelson's ship, the *Captain*, was
a 74, and after being engaged with the Spanish
flagship and others, came into close action with
the *San Nicolas*, 84, and the *San Josef*, 112, both of
which were captured by boarding, Nelson and his
comrades passing over from one ship to the other.
Collingwood in the *Excellent* took a fine part in this
episode, as did Troubridge in the *Culloden*, in the
great result, but the glory of the day was Nelson's,
and Jervis gladly recognized the worth of such
splendid disobedience. The merit of the achieve-
ment was that Nelson had realized the small power
of resistance possessed by the Spaniards, and knew
what risks he could run. He had said, "The
Spanish fleet is ill-manned, and worse officered,
I fancy." The result of the victory has already been
indicated. It defeated the combined purpose of
the French and Spanish fleets, and destroyed all
immediate prospects of invading England. It was
on the 24th of July in the same year that Nelson lost
his right arm in the attack on Santa Cruz, Teneriffe,
an operation which ended in failure.

We come now to that remarkable illustration of
the imagination, the enterprise, the daring and the
moral courage of Bonaparte, the expedition to
Egypt in 1798. All his plans were laid during the
period when we had abandoned the Mediterranean,

and when the pathway to Egypt and to his ambitions in India lay open. It was known that a great armament was preparing at Toulon, and that the Spaniards had some twenty-five ships ready for an enterprise at Cadiz. St Vincent was blockading the latter port, but detached Nelson, anticipating the views of the Admiralty, to observe Toulon. Nelson, unfortunately having with him only three sail of the line, three frigates and a sloop—for the previous administration had not provided enough ships and St Vincent could spare no more—looked into Toulon on the 17th of May.

Then arose a gale in which his flagship, the *Vanguard*, was dismasted. She was towed and piloted by her consorts for shelter and repair to San Pietro, Sardinia, while the three frigates and the sloop had departed to Gibraltar and were not seen by Nelson for months. By extraordinary exertions, the *Vanguard* was refitted within four days, but when the three ships came again off Toulon, they found that the great French armament, which they had seen, had departed. Admiral Brueys, with twelve sail of the line, and a number of frigates, accompanied by a cloud of transports, had put to sea on the 19th, favoured by the wind that had blown Nelson off, and after taking possession of Malta and being joined by convoys from Genoa, Ajaccio and Civita Vecchia, had proceeded on his course to Egypt. We cannot resist the conclusion that if St Vincent could have provided Nelson with a sufficient force, it would have been easy to prevent the several sections of the invading army from joining forces. The reinforcement did not come until the 7th of June, nearly three weeks after the French had put to sea, Troubridge arriving with ten 74's and the 50-gun ship *Leander*.

Now descended upon Nelson the grievous disability of the want of frigates to act as the eyes and ears of his fleet. He had no swift cruisers or destroyers, no aeroplane and no wireless telegraphy to help him. Only the speechless sea surrounded him, and he passed within the close vicinity of the enemy without knowing it. The French were well aware of the perils that surrounded them in this stealtby enterprise. They were indeed within an ace of terrible disaster. Sulkowski, who was in a position to know the mind of Bonaparte, wrote in alarm at the critical situation which would confront the vast army if a superior enemy should appear, and compel them to fight with their vessels encumbered with baggage and military stores, and having to defend a vast and incoherent convoy.

When the French arrived before Alexandria on the 1st of July, and learned that Nelson had left the port on the previous day, they thanked their stars for escape from the perils that had menaced them.

"The presence of the English had shadowed our horizon," wrote Vivant Denon, who had gone ahead of the fleet in the *Junon*; "when I remembered that three days before we had deplored the calms that held us back, and that without them we should have fallen amid the enemy's fleet, I vowed myself thenceforward to fatalism and commended myself to the star of Bonaparte."

It was realized that Nelson might return at any hour, and therefore the troops were sent precipitately ashore, while the squadron, unable to enter the port, and fearing the risk of going to Corfu, went into Aboukir Bay, there to await the onslaught of Nelson. Such was the invasion of Egypt, which ended in the destruction of a fleet and the surrender of an army. After his visit to Alexandria, Nelson, still seeking the French, had gone to Syracuse, and there, with the persuasion of force, and a letter from Acton, the Neapolitan Prime Minister, had secured the revictualling of his fleet, notwithstanding the Neapolitan treaty with France. It was during this long cruise that he imparted to his captains— his "band of brothers," as he called them—his ideas as to his plan of action on meeting the enemy at sea or at anchor. It was in the latter situation that Nelson found the fleet of Admiral Brueys, lying in an irregular line about three miles from the shore in shallow water. The French fleet was nominally superior to the English, but in effect it was not so, because Nelson's ships were in a state of hard discipline, while the reverse was the case with the French.

The battle began on the 1st of August, just as the sun touched the horizon. Nelson's plan was to overpower the French van and centre, and, while the *Goliath*, followed by four other ships, passed inside the French line, raking the ships with a terrific fire, Nelson in the *Vanguard*, followed by several other ships passed outside. Thus by a tempest of fire the French van was crushed. A tremendous conflict took place in the centre, where was the French admiral (who was killed) in the *Orient*, 120, with the *Franklin* and *Tonnant*, both 80's. The *Bellerophon* and *Majestic* suffered very severely, but the French flagship blew up, a terrible disaster for the French. In this way the victory was won. In addition to the *Orient*, the *Timoléon*, being driven ashore, was burnt by her crew, and nine sail of the line were captured. Never in modern war had there been a victory so complete. The *Guillaume Tell* and *Généreux* were the only French line ships that escaped, and both of them were subsequently captured.

Nelson arrived at Naples in a blaze of glory, which had the result of placing him under a shadow, the personal reasons for which must be sought in

the biographies. It is impossible to regard the
subsequent handling of the fleet with much satisfaction. If a strong force had been left in the
Eastern Mediterranean, the grip on the French army
in Egypt would have been tighter, and Napoleon
might not have returned. If the whole fleet had
been concentrated in the Western basin, there
might well have been no need for Trafalgar. Bruix,
with twenty-five sail of the line, including four of
110 guns and two of 80, left Brest, under the nose
of Bridport—who, besides, had insufficient force—
and appeared in the Mediterranean. But our ships
were scattered, and he was not interfered with.
He reached Toulon, ranged along the Italian coast
to assist the French armies, and in due course returned to Brest, carrying with him a somewhat
unwilling Spanish squadron.

Pitt was successful in creating a second coalition of
the Powers against France, and the year 1799 opened
with splendid prospects. But Austria wavered,
and when the Peace of Lunéville was signed in
February, 1801, the great coalition came to an end,
leaving us without an ally on the continent. The
naval events of the period cannot detain us. They
were neither important nor decisive. Efforts were
scattered, but in the many combined operations, the
Navy always did its duty well. It was sometimes
the object that was at fault, and the soldiery that

failed. However, we took Malta, defended Elba, and at length landed Sir Ralph Abercromby's army to act effectively in Egypt. The Northern Coalition, in which Russia, Prussia, Denmark and Sweden were ranged against us, was in pursuit of Bonaparte's aims of a "Continental System," which should strike at our trade by closing the ports of Europe against our ships. Therefore, in March, 1801, Sir Hyde Parker, with Nelson as second in command, went with a fleet to compel Denmark and Sweden to desist from this exclusive policy. In the attack on Copenhagen Nelson once more showed his supreme qualities as a fighter of battles. Parker relinquished the critical business to him, and issued orders for recall, which Nelson might regard as permissive if he desired. Nelson, looking with the telescope to his blind eye, could not see the signal. It was a desperate business, and Nelson having taken possession of his prizes, hastened to withdraw. The object was attained, and the Northern Coalition, or Armed Neutrality as it was called, ceased to exist.

There was one other engagement in the war to which allusion may be made. This was the double action of Sir James Saumarez, which defeated a new scheme of naval concentration at Cadiz. Linois coming from Toulon with three ships, and knowing his opponent was before him in superior force, took

refuge at Algeciras.   There Saumarez attacked him
in most gallant style, and not without loss.   Then
Linois, with a Spanish squadron in his company,
put to sea, and ran out into the ocean.   There
Saumarez again attacked, and two big Spanish
ships were destroyed, with a loss of 2000 men.

The naval situation was hopeless for Bonaparte,
now First Consul.   Everywhere triumphant on
the continent, the British Navy had proved both
sword and buckler to the Power which stood in the
pathway of his ambition beyond the sea.   Respite
was sought by both countries from the terrible strain
of the war, an overmastering desire for peace existed
among the peoples, and after long negotiations
the transient Peace of Amiens was signed on the
27th of March, 1802.

CHAPTER XVI

IDEAS AND PLANS OF BONAPARTE

THE Peace of Amiens was merely a truce, and
there was yet need for a supreme effort on the part
of Bonaparte if all his projects against England were
not to fail.   In this country few people were well
pleased with the settlement that had been arrived
at.   Addington had succeeded Pitt, and the nation
was not satisfied to find that after so many sacrifices

their enemy remained unshorn by reverses in the war. France was, in fact, ringing with the noise of a diplomatic triumph. Elba and Piedmont were annexed; the States of Parma were occupied; the Italian Republic was Bonaparte's; Germany was partitioned; Holland was a vassal; Austria was crushed and broken; Switzerland had been brought under the protection of France; and Louisiana had been wrung from Spain.

There were, it is true, but few means for undertaking maritime war. The remnant of the fleet was dispersed, and the expedition to San Domingo had exhausted many resources. The schemes in the West Indies were unrealized; and the finances were in a shocking state. But nothing had occurred to darken the First Consul's dream of a world dominion. The Treaty of Lunéville, which was not affected by the Peace of Amiens, had freed him from continental embarrassments. The political mission of Sebastiani, and that of General Decaen as Captain-General of the French forces in India, had revealed his purposes. But he had realized that not for ten years to come could he hope to muster a fleet that could be fairly matched with the British. He hoped to accomplish his purposes in alliance with Spain and Holland, and in all his invasionary schemes he had counted on rebellion in Ireland as a chief factor for success.

With the exception of Trinidad and Ceylon we
had surrendered our conquests, but the provision
that we should restore Malta to the Knights of
St John, virtually handing it over to France, was
peculiarly obnoxious to the nation and the Navy.
Whitworth, our ambassador in Paris, spoke of the
island as the " watch-tower of Egypt," and to Nelson
it was " a most important out-work of India."
Neither Addington in 1803, nor Pitt after his return
to power in 1804, would tolerate the idea of surrendering Malta.   The First Consul knew how little cause
we had to be satisfied, and dreaded that we might
seize the initiative, which he regarded as the beginning, middle and end of warfare.   Peace, he said,
was only conditional so long as we could throw our
Navy and our gold into the scale.   Most French
historians, including Thiers and Albert Sorel, lay
the responsibility for the new outbreak of war at our
door.

It is certain that the First Consul was exasperated
by what had occurred.   It was reported to him that
the Navy, after its long efforts, was in a very bad
state.   No one could remember seeing it in a condition so deplorable.   The vast expenditure on the
Army had diverted supplies from it.   The ships
were rotten and reeking with disease ; the officers
demoralized ; and the men mutinous and unpaid.
The ravages of revolution and the effects of disastrous

war had wasted it. The Jacobin spirit ranged the men against their officers, and the zealous few strove long in vain to break through the tangle of corruption and fraud. Toulon was exhausted, and stores and magazines were empty. Wood was wanting for the building of ships. Brest was in a state almost equally deplorable, and there, through treachery, a ship of the line, the *Patriote*, was burnt. " Il manque de tout," said Caffarelli, the naval prefect, and when war broke out everything remained to be done.

The First Consul never understood well the conduct of naval affairs. He thought it was possible to dare, and yet not to risk. He strove with all his might to replace sloth by energy and neglect by activity, but he could neither give the fleet the will to strike nor for many months conjure away the profound maladies that afflicted it.

The British fleet had also gone through a trying period, but its officers were men of high confidence, and the cheery courage with which the winter blockades were borne was proof enough of the quality of the men. There was waste and corruption in the dockyards, under the Navy Board, and St Vincent brought about the appointment of a Royal Commission to inquire into irregularities, frauds and abuses, which was followed by another commission " for Revising and Digesting the Civil Affairs of the

Navy." But the Navy had been kept practically on a war footing during the peace, and had never been better found nor better supplied, nor had the men ever been better fed or clothed. At the outbreak of war we had 39 sail of the line and many frigates, while the French had only thirteen available, and those in a bad state. But our number was insufficient, and when Lord Barham went to the Admiralty in the next year, he was utterly astonished at the little care there had been, in this material matter, in "maintaining the empire of the sea."

Our conduct of the war was based on the system of blockade, and the blockade extended from Toulon to Flushing. Nelson was off Toulon with nine sail of the line in July, 1803, and he had everything to provide, including the establishment of a base at Maddalena. Latouche-Tréville, the French admiral, was a man of surprising vigour and initiative, and was rapidly reviving the fleet. Nelson's principle was not to hold the French in Toulon, but to get them out to sea, where he might defeat them. At Brest, gallant Cornwallis rode out many a gale at his station off the Black Rocks, bearing up sometimes for Torbay for refit and repair, and organizing a most efficient system of reliefs. Like Nelson he would have liked to meet the French, but in those narrow waters there was no better method than a close blockade on St Vincent's

system. Some French ships returning from San
Domingo got into Ferrol and Corunna, and those
ports were blockaded by the statesmanlike Pellew
and the vigilant Cochrane, and a close watch was
kept also upon Rochefort and Lorient. The blockade
was extended by Lord Keith in the Downs, who
watched the coasts from Havre to the Texel.

There was no certainty as to the actual purposes
of Bonaparte. Cornwallis thought every contin-
gency must be kept in view. Lord Melville, First
Lord of the Admiralty, feared that ships might
break out from the ocean ports, join the Toulon
squadron, and endeavour to crush Nelson. Nelson
also inclined to this view, though sometimes he
thought that a mission to Ireland was intended.
British officers never attached much importance
to the invasionary flotilla of flat-bottomed boats,
which was being assembled in the ports. They
did an immense amount of damage to it, by
courageous inshore attacks and cutting out expeditions which constitute a dramatic page of the
romance of the Navy. Under the pressure of the
blockade Bonaparte's own plans constantly changed.
There was a time when he said, " Let us be masters
of the Channel for six hours and we shall be
masters of the world." Ganteaume, commanding
the squadron at Brest, told him this enterprise of
evasion would be " extremely bold and extremely

perilous." When Forfait wrote to the First Consul describing the redoubtable character of the flotillas, Admiral Decrès, Minister of Marine, said his assertions were monstrous and absurd paradoxes, coming from one who had never left the shore nor heard the whistle of a bullet.

In December, 1803, and again in 1804, Bonaparte was urging Admiral Latouche-Tréville to deceive Nelson into thinking an expedition to Egypt was intended, and then to come round and join forces he was to release at Cadiz and Rochefort, and with them to appear in the Channel. But Latouche-Tréville died in August, 1804, and Villeneuve, who replaced him, had orders to leave Toulon, effect a junction with the Rochefort squadron, cruise to the West Indies, seize our colonies, proceed to Surinam and return to relieve the blockade of Ferrol. Fresh orders gave directions that the Toulon and Rochefort squadrons should go westward independently. Nelson foresaw these possibilities and others, and said, "Whatever may be their destination I shall certainly follow, be it even to the East Indies." But on the 14th December, 1804, Villeneuve wrote to Napoleon deploring the weakness of his squadron, and declaring it to be unfit to go to sea. The truth was that the stringency of the blockade forbade the co-operation of the French admirals owing to the doubt as to their escape and the time at which such escape might take place.

The first move in the game was made in January, 1805, by Admiral Missiessy, who escaped from Rochefort during the temporary absence of Sir Thomas Graves, and went to the West Indies, pursued by Admiral Cochrane. He saw nothing of Villeneuve, and, without accomplishing anything, returned, and had the good fortune to reach Rochefort unchallenged. Villeneuve had meanwhile given detailed instructions to his fleet, which promised decisive action, and he essayed to leave his port on the 18th of January, 1805. But the wind proved foul, ships were damaged, and he returned, to write a desponding letter to Napoleon. He said that ships such as his, improperly manned, encumbered with troops, losing masts, sails and rigging in any wind, and occupied in repairing in fair weather the damage done in foul, were useless for any enterprise. By this time the Spaniards were against us, for Captain Graham Moore, brother of Sir John Moore, had seized the Spanish treasure ships, on the 5th of October, 1804, and on the 4th of January, 1805, Decrès and Gravina signed the secret convention between France and Spain.

Villeneuve's despondency appalled Napoleon, and orders of 2nd March placed the whole intended operation under the orders of Ganteaume at Brest. That admiral was to leave the port with twenty-one sail of the line and six frigates, to elude the blockading squadron, attack Calder off Ferrol, signal to Gourdon, who was there, to join him with the French and Spanish ships, to proceed to Martinique, where he was to join Villeneuve and Missiessy, and then to return with forty sail of the line, and appear off Boulogne, where he would receive further orders. Ganteaume was quite ready to issue from the port, but the squadron of Cornwallis was outside, and he was on the horns of a dilemma. " A victory in these circumstances would lead to nothing. Have but one object—to execute your mission. Go out without fighting." Such were Bonaparte's orders. The Admiral remained in port and awaited the opportunity that never came. His inability to get away was the determining factor of the situation.

At Toulon Villeneuve was fortunate. On the 30th of March he issued from his port, and making a fair passage, arrived at Martinique on the 14th May, there to learn that Missiessy had returned and that nothing had been seen of Ganteaume. Then orders were issued to Villeneuve to assume chief command. He was to wait thirty-five days at Martinique, and if Ganteaume did not arrive, was to return, gather to his flag fifteen French and Spanish ships from Ferrol, and Ganteaume's twenty-one from Brest, and thus assume command of a fleet of fifty-six sail of the line.

Nelson's system of a loose form of blockade had failed to keep the French at Toulon, which indeed he had not desired. A greater failure had been his inability to bring them to action when they left the port. But his movements must be judged in the light of Pitt's policy at the time. The Minister feared that Sicily might fall into the hands of the French, and was despatching for its succour an expedition, under Craig, which, when he heard of it, constituted a grave embarrassment for Nelson's position. Nelson's mind was turned to the East. When, however, he definitely learned which course the French admiral had taken, he immediately pursued in a manner that was a triumph of seamanlike skill. It has sometimes been alleged that he was decoyed away, but nothing could be further from the fact. His object was to bring his adversary to action, and he took his westward course with a well-defined strategic object.

CHAPTER XVII

THE CAMPAIGN OF TRAFALGAR

WHEN Nelson went westward it was with a definite knowledge of the course that Villeneuve had taken. The interest of a great commerce lay in the West Indies, and it was necessary either to defeat the French in that region or to drive them thence. Nelson said that if the islands fell, the people would be so clamorous for peace that we should humble ourselves. His force was numerically inferior, and his adversary had a full month's start of him, but he had weighed every point in the game. At home great apprehension prevailed owing to uncertainty as to the position and movements of the fleets. Colonel Robert Craufurd told the Commons that our naval forces might be drawn away to the West Indies, and that the enemy, hastening back to Europe, might gain temporary command of the Channel, capture the anchorage in the Downs, and bring the army over. It is recorded that Mr Bragge, Secretary at War, smiled at the idea, and certainly St Vincent and the sea officers entertained no such apprehensions. They knew that strategy and adequate force would make the operation impossible. Nevertheless there were sundry alarms, and on one occasion a quantity of burning straw, mistaken for a beacon, brought the forces of Derbyshire and West Yorkshire under arms.

The protean character of Napoleon's plans has been suggested in the last chapter. They followed the lines of least resistance. Many of them were dictated during his triumphant progress through Italy, when he placed the iron crown of Lombardy on his head, and, intoxicated with power, fancied

he could move his fleets like pieces on a chess-board.
Events like the return of Missiessy to Rochefort,
without having accomplished anything, though pro-
foundly disconcerting, never shook his optimism,
and he was ever ready with a new combination.
He made a constant appeal to the glories of a successful campaign against England. "You hold in your
hands the destinies of the world," he wrote to
Ganteaume, and again, "We shall have avenged
six centuries of insults and shame; never for a
greater object have my seamen and soldiers exposed
their lives."

Concerning Napoleon's military preparations for
the famous descent upon England, there was a
division of opinion in the French army, and Berthier
considered the operation extremely risky. That was
the general opinion of the sea officers, who, however,
did not always dare to give utterance to their views.
By the losses the invasion flotilla had suffered during
its assembly, and the incapacity with which it had
been handled, the improbability of its ever serving
its purpose seemed to have been demonstrated. The
harbours had been improved, but it would have been
impossible for the flotilla to put to sea in less than
two tides. Although every detail was set forth on
paper, it is doubtful whether more than 90,000 troops
were ever assembled. Napoleon, in 1805, expressed
very uncertain views as to the time which would be

required for the passage : to Decrès, six hours (June), twelve hours (August), fourteen days (September) ; to Villeneuve, three days (May), four or five days (July), twenty-four hours (August) ; to Ganteaume, three days (July). But, in effect, Napoleon had learned that a stealthy passage within a few hours would be impossible, and the combination of fleets upon a vast scale, directed to their concentration off Boulogne, entered into his plans.

In his later years the Emperor was accustomed to assert that he had never been in earnest in this expedition, but it was usual with him thus to seek escape from the obloquy of schemes which had failed. There had come indeed a time when he had questioned the possibility of success. In such case, he said to Bourrienne, " I shall make my Army of England the Army of the East and go to Egypt." Egypt was the outpost of India. " Europe is a mere mole-hill : it is only in the East, where there are 600,000,000 of human beings, that there have been vast empires and mighty revolutions." Madame de Rémusat, Miot de Mélito, General Hulot, Lucchesini and Metternich all incline to doubt whether there was any real intention of putting the plan of invasion into execution. But the great expenditure upon preparations for the enterprise, the minute and exhaustive care displayed in many parts of the organization, the vast importance that Napoleon

attached to success, the earnestness that breathes
in every line he wrote concerning the scheme, and
more than all the meaninglessness which otherwise
would have marked his plans, all forbid us to doubt
that, against England, he had staked everything
upon the success of the enterprise. The invasion
of England, which blocked the pathway to his world
ambition, was one of the great objects he had set
before himself, and we cannot question that the
flotilla was intended to transport to our shores those
troops which he hoped would dictate peace at the
capital.

The Navy was to shatter the fabric of the great
imperial dream. The situation was this. Cornwallis was blockading Brest, where Ganteaume had
twenty-one sail of the line, Rear-Admiral Stirling
off Rochefort was holding tight Allemand (who had
succeeded Missiessy), Sir Robert Calder was off
Ferrol blockading Gourdon and Grandallana, and
Collingwood was off Cadiz, with some ships off Cartagena. When it became known, from despatches sent
home by Nelson in the *Curieux* brig, that the combined fleets of France and Spain under command of
Villeneuve and Gravina were actually homeward
bound, Lord Barham, that most able administrator,
who had succeeded Lord Melville at the Admiralty,
and his colleagues ordered a certain redistribution of
forces. There was not an adequate strength for every

station, and consequently Stirling was to leave his post before Rochefort and reinforce Calder off Ferrol, who thereupon, with fifteen sail of the line and other vessels, was to stretch thirty or forty leagues to the westward with the object of intercepting the enemy. Stirling's departure released Allemand, who made a most adventurous cruise with the object of meeting Villeneuve, but the *Didon*, carrying Villeneuve's despatches, was captured by the *Phœnix*, and the meeting did not take place.

Calder met the combined squadron on the 22nd July, about 49 leagues west of Ferrol, in a drifting mist and endeavoured to engage the enemy's rear and centre. This attack was parried, and then fog descended upon the combatants. Two Spanish ships, which had suffered a good deal, drifted into the midst of Calder's fleet and were captured. The action was creditable, though not either conclusive or decisive. Calder thought well of what he had accomplished, but he failed to renew the action on the following day, being under apprehension that the ships at Ferrol would join Villeneuve and crush him. " He appears," wrote Nelson, " to have had the ships of Ferrol more in his head than the squadron in sight." For this slackness Calder was greatly blamed, and was subsequently tried by court martial, " for not having done his utmost to renew the said engagement, and to take every ship of the enemy."

The latter he had not done, and could not have done. After the action he proceeded to join Cornwallis off Brest, while Villeneuve, having first found an anchorage at Vigo, entered the outer bay of Ferrol on the 1st of August. The combined fleet had returned in a terrible condition from the effects of scarcity, bad weather and disease. The admiral was himself ill, and was deeply impressed by the fact that Calder had attacked him with inferior force, while his own captains had known nothing of fleet tactics, and the fleet was the laughing-stock of Europe.

Nelson had expected Villeneuve to proceed to the Mediterranean, and therefore shaped his course to Gibraltar, where he arrived on the 19th July, but on hearing that the French were steering a more northerly course, he proceeded, with eleven sail of the line, to join Cornwallis off Brest, who gave him an order to proceed to Spithead, where he struck his flag. The situation had now become critical. Napoleon was at Boulogne, and all seemed ready for the great enterprise. Neither Lord Barham at the Admiralty nor Cornwallis off Brest knew what was the immediate object of Villeneuve. It was possible that he might seek to enter the Mediterranean. Accordingly Cornwallis, on the 16th August, instructed Sir Robert Calder to take under his command twenty of the ships off Brest (where only eighteen were left) and to proceed off Ferrol in order to prevent the combined fleet from putting to sea. This division of the fleet has been adversely criticised, and Napoleon described it as an *insigne bêtise*—a signal blunder—but Cornwallis had measured the risk, and knew that off Ferrol the squadron might check the enemy whether he went south or north. Napoleon himself was guilty of an *insigne bêtise* at Marengo, where he divided his forces by detaching Desaix and another general, and narrowly escaped losing the battle.

But Villeneuve, with the great fleet, left Ferrol before the squadron detached by Cornwallis could reach the station. Napoleon told Ganteaume that Villeneuve's apparent intention was to pass through the Raz de Sein and enter Brest harbour, but Ganteaume was given supreme authority. He was to permit no such delay, but with 50 ships was to proceed into the Channel and appear before Boulogne. Villeneuve's fleet began to get under way from the outer bay of Ferrol on the 10th of August, but was not clear of the coast until the 14th. As is well known, instead of doing what Napoleon had desired, the dispirited and discouraged admiral turned to the south and entered Cadiz. He had been alarmed at what he thought the approach of Cornwallis, and declared that he had no confidence in his own fleet, that he believed he had freedom of action, that the situation had changed since he had received his orders, and that he saw no prospect of success. In this supreme moment of Napoleon's career, the pressure of British sea power, the crushing weight of our superiority, dashed the cup of success from his lips. It was the most bitter moment of his career, and his exaspera-tion at the failure was terrible to behold. "What a fleet!" he exclaimed, "What sacrifices for nothing! What an Admiral! All hope is gone!" Immedi-ately he broke up his camp at Boulogne and marched on the 28th of August for the Danube, to win his first signal success against the Austrians at Ulm on the very day on which his fleet was destroyed at Trafalgar.

Nelson left Spithead in the *Victory* on the 15th of September, and assumed command of the fleet off Cadiz on the 28th. He hoped for reinforcements. "Numbers only can annihilate," he wrote, "and therefore I hope the Admiralty will send the fixed force as soon as possible." He estimated that the allies would have forty-six sail of the line, and hoped himself to have not less than forty, and with this expectation issued to the fleet on the 9th of October his famous and masterly Memorandum on the tactics to be employed in the coming battle, which he had discussed with his friends before leaving England. This "Nelson touch," as he called it, is the most ad-mirable exposition of tactical principles ever penned. It would "bring forward a pell-mell battle, and that is what I want." Mr J. R. Thursfield has very ably disengaged the great principles of the plan, which, he says, "was an exceedingly subtle, and not less original, combination of the several ideas of concentration on the rear, of complete freedom of action for the second in command (Collingwood), of containing the enemy's van and centre until the business of twelve sail of the enemy was seen to be so far advanced that its interruption was no longer to be feared, and, above all, of the concealment of his own intentions until the last moment, so as to confuse the enemy's mind by not letting him know where and how the attack of the weather line was to be delivered."

The battle of Trafalgar, fought on the 21st of October, cannot be described here. It was a decisive and immortal victory the incidents of which have been recounted by many pens, and whose splendours are in all our histories. Nelson was fortunate in his death, for he fell in the hour of his triumph. The numbers were not what he had expected, for the allies had thirty-three sail of the line, and he only twenty-seven—twelve in his own weather line, and fifteen in the lee line of Colling-wood. The engagement was fought in light and variable airs which made it impossible for the ships to assume the definite formations which Nelson had anticipated, and the allied line began to wear at the beginning of the action, altering course to return to

Cadiz. But the principles which the famous seaman had laid down were applied, and the great object was won. Eighteen of the enemy's ships were taken, of which three were recaptured on the following days. The rest fled, but other captures came to us, notably four ships under Dumanoir which escaped and were brought to action by Sir Richard Strachan on the 4th November off Cape Ortegal. In all, 22 ships were lost to the allies, and of the eleven which escaped into Cadiz, not one ever again went to sea to serve as a ship of war.

CHAPTER XVIII

THE FRUITS OF VICTORY

THE battle of Trafalgar gave us command of the sea in the sense that thenceforward we possessed the power to control our own sea communications, and in a general, though not an absolute sense, to control those of our adversaries. The allied fleet had been annihilated, but in the age of wooden sailing ships, as we have many times seen in the preceding chapters, there existed a power of re-cuperation from disasters, such as cannot exist in times when ships of the line, or as we now call them battleships or battle-cruisers, each cost much more than £2,000,000. Napoleon, in effect, set about the building of many new ships of the line, not only in France, but in the ports of the North Sea and Italy, which came under his sway. They were not much employed, because it was easier to build ships than to provide capable officers and contented men, and, many of the ships being constructed of green timber, soon rotted into uselessness.

The Berlin Decree against our commerce was the sign of the naval failure. It was not possible for us to blockade every place which became a source of danger to trade, and swarms of privateers issued from the French ports, and from ports in the West Indies and Mauritius, and the Dutch harbours of Java and Sumatra. Thus a great strain was put upon the Navy in many parts of the world, lasting up to the very end of the long war. The result was a considerable increase in the number of sea-going ships, beginning in 1806, and the numbers remained high in every year until 1815, when for the first time they fell below the establishment of 1805: 485, as compared with 508. At the same time, the number of ships building, which in 1805 had been 81, rose to 131 in 1806, and the figure was 108 in 1807 and 111 in 1808. It did not fall below the figure of 1805 until 1810, and it rose to 110 in 1813. Necessarily also, in the years following Trafalgar, the Navy attained its greatest number of officers and men up to the peace of 1815.

The attack upon our commerce by privateers and light squadrons in those years caused trouble to our merchants, but all experience shows that commerce-destroying never has been and never can be a primary object in war. During the twenty years of fighting in the French Revolutionary and Napoleonic struggle our annual loss in shipping was only about 2·36 per cent. We captured in privateers 41,000 seamen, and of war vessels engaged in commerce-destruction we took about five for every 21 merchant vessels lost. During this period the volume of our maritime trade more than doubled, while the French mercantile flag practically disappeared from the seas. It would be wrong therefore to attach high importance to the operations of commerce-destroyers either before or after Trafalgar.

Some notes may be added upon the activity of warships in the years subsequent to Trafalgar. The Admiralty relaxed the strictness of the blockade of Brest in the winter of 1805–6, and Vice-Admiral Leissègues, with five sail of the line, and Rear-Admiral Willaumez with six, slipped away, the former to be defeated by Sir John Duckworth off San Domingo on the 6th February, 1806, and the latter, after an adventurous cruise in West Indian and North Atlantic waters, to have his squadron broken up in action with various British forces. When Napoleon, in 1809, decided to venture a strong

squadron composed of ships from Brest and Rochefort on a cruise to the West Indies, the armament
was driven into the Basque Roads and there attacked with fireships under the orders of Lord
Cochrane, afterwards Earl of Dundonald, and ruined,
though Lord Gambier, in superior command, interfered to check the completeness of the operation.
That we were not always able to control the enemy's
communications was shown by the passage of Allemand from Rochefort to Toulon, with five sail of the
line, in 1808, when Sir Richard Strachan, who was
blockading the former port, was away revictualling
at his rendezvous, and also by the cruise of Ganteaume,
who was then commanding at Toulon, to revictual
the garrison at Corfu, and his unimpeded return to
his port.

But our own communications were in every case
secure. Oversea possessions are the fruit of sea
power, though in nearly every case the fruit must
be gathered by the exercise of military force. When
war broke out in 1803 we re-occupied the Dutch West
Indian islands, which had been surrendered at the
peace, and in 1804 we occupied Surinam. The Cape
was re-occupied in 1806, and in the following years
Curaçao, Martinique, Cayenne, Guadeloupe, Mauritius, Amboyna, the Moluccas and Java fell into our
hands.

The sea power which had been won at Trafalgar

was nowhere better exercised than during the
Peninsular War, where its potent influence was
" silent," to use Admiral Mahan's word, though
signally effective. If a superior hostile fleet had
stood in our pathway in the Channel, the Bay of
Biscay or on the coast of Portugal at the time, Spain
would have lain at the feet of the conqueror. It
was the fleet that gave strategical mobility to the
Army. Wellesley's expeditionary force reached the
Peninsula without let or hindrance, and was free
to land at Vigo, Oporto or Mondego Bay, as the
general might choose. Sir Charles Cotton's squadron
was the base for its communications and support.
When Moore had advanced on Salamanca and the
upper Douro, finding his retirement on Portugal
cut off and his army endangered, he made his
heroic march through the mountains of Galicia to
reach the fleet, which lay at Coruña ready for the
embarkation of the troops. The Army was in the
Peninsula by virtue of sea power, and that power was
its refuge and its link with its home-base throughout
the war. The lines of Torres Vedras owed their endurance to the sea power that was behind them, the
effect of which Wellesley had fully understood. In
the winter after Talavera and Busaco, when he was
forced upon the defensive, he established his im-
pregnable position behind these lines in the peninsula
which separates the lower Tagus from the Atlantic.

The strength of Torres Vedras was rooted in the support of the fleet in the Tagus, and the communications which that fleet maintained with England. When at length the great advance began which carried the Army from the basin of the Douro to Gascony and Languedoc, Wellesley, finding that "at each remove he dragged a lengthening chain," shifted his base, by means of sea power, from the Tagus to the Basque provinces. The transports sailed round from Lisbon to Santander, furnishing a fine illustration of the influence of sea command in the creation of an alternative naval base, and a great factor in military success. Up to the very end of the war the fleet was the base for the operations of the Army. The admirals felt no such anxiety for the safety of the transports as perturbed the soul of Nelson, in the case of Craig's expedition, in the times before Trafalgar, when the French were still powerful and active at sea.

England was now the mistress of the seas, and her prosperity grew by leaps and bounds, though it was prosperity generally for the rich and not always for the poor. On the continent, the French armies were driven back across the Pyrenees and the Rhine, the foemen advanced, Paris surrendered, and the Emperor abdicated. But this series of triumphs had been marred for us by the outbreak of a new struggle across the Atlantic, which arose from the Berlin and Milan Decrees of Napoleon, the retaliatory Orders in Council, and the non-intercourse policy of the United States. Some incidents in the war of 1812 gave a rather rude awakening to the British Navy, which, when war was declared, was at the very zenith of its fame, rich in the inherited experience of its overthrow of the historic maritime Powers, and brought to a high standard of efficiency by warfare that had continued almost without interruption for eighteen years.

It seemed, in certain untoward events of this war, as if a pigmy was wrestling successfully with a giant, and the giant was aroused to a knowledge of his deficiencies by his discomfitures. The story goes that Nelson once saw an American squadron in European waters—perhaps that of Captain Richard Dale in 1801, Captain Richard Morris in 1802–3, or Captain Edward Preble in 1803—and that he uttered a forecast in these words : '' There is in the handling of these Transatlantic ships a nucleus of trouble for the Navy of Great Britain.'' The trouble was, indeed, in the handling of individual ships, usually in frigate actions, for there was no general engagement, and the impression created by a few misfortunes was out of all proportion to their importance.

In a volume which is concerned with the building up of the Empire through the influence of the Navy, and inferentially with its conservation by the same means, some evidences of apparent weakening in the spirit of the service may well deserve attention. Possibly some slackness arose from over-confidence, and may have been due in a measure to easy content in great things achieved. The admirals at least seem to have thought that Nelson's Memorandum—which not all of them understood—was the last word upon tactics. Some captains were probably so intent upon the externals of efficiency that the essentials escaped them, and gunnery declined. A great body of the men were prime seamen, but they had been rigorously treated, and a considerable number of the class had gone over to America and joined the United States Navy, to which they had imparted a good deal of its efficiency. Those who remained were brought into association, owing to the enormous demand for men, with the offscourings of gaols, gathered in by the press. "Convicts, vagabonds, thieves not brought to justice from lenity, smugglers, White Boys, suspected Irish during the rebellion, all who from loss of character could not procure employment, the idle and the worthless," wrote Captain Anselm Griffiths—"all was fish that came to the net."

History is rich in examples of defeats inflicted upon old experience and tried capacity by antagonists whose power has not been suspected. The vast fleet of Xerxes was annihilated at " rock bound Salamis," and his seasoned veterans were utterly routed by their despised foe at Platæa. But Lysander captured an Athenian fleet at Ægos-potami, and the Athenians never fully recovered from the great naval disaster at Syracuse. The military predominance of Sparta ended with the defeat of her hardened legions at Leuctra. Rome fell before the barbarians. The magnificent in-fantry of Spain were routed at Rocroi. Burgoyne's army surrendered at Saratoga. The model army of Prussia, which had been trained in the military methods of the great Frederick, was vanquished at Jena. And coming to modern times, how few there were who foresaw that the mighty army of Russia would be worsted by the young army of Japan, or that the forces of the Balkan States would over-throw the formidable legions of the Turk ? These facts have only a distant relation to our incidental disasters in 1812–14, but they should be borne in mind as warnings by maritime nations which may be tempted into the complacent belief that they may have a privilege of predominance at sea, or may suffer themselves to decline from want of stimulus, in the quietude of a long peace.

Of the events of the war with the United States there is little room to speak. The Americans pos-sessed no ships of the line, but they had three splendid 44-gun frigates, the *United States*, *Constitution* and *President*, which were superior to any frigates in the British Navy. On the 19th August, 1812, the *Constitution*, after a most desperate fight with the British 38-gun frigate *Guerrière*, reduced that vessel to helplessness by sheer weight of fire, and captured her in such a condition that she had to be destroyed. On the 25th October, the *United States*, after a hard-fought action, captured the British frigate *Macedonian*, to which in every respect save speed she was greatly superior. Moreover she had a first-rate captain in the person of Stephen Decatur. Four days later the 38-gun frigate *Java* was captured by the *Constitution*, and there were other captures. The most famous action of the war was that of the 1st June, 1813, between the British frigate *Shannon*, Captain Philip Broke, and the American frigate *Chesapeake*, Captain James Lawrence, being vessels of about equal power commanded by equally valiant men ; an action which showed that the fighting quality of the British Navy still existed and still could dominate. The *Shannon* had been brought to a high state of efficiency, and the *Chesapeake*, as her commander reported, had her crew " in fine spirits." The victory of the British ship was complete, and her antagonist was carried by boarding. The gallant American captain was killed. There was fighting on the great lakes with varying fortune, and the Navy played a large part in the operations which brought about the surrender of Washington, and in the attacks on Baltimore and New Orleans, which were ineffective. Peace was signed at Ghent on the 21st of December, 1814.

Our long struggle with the Revolution and the Empire came to an end when Napoleon for the second time surrendered, on board the *Bellerophon*, Captain Maitland, and peace was concluded at Paris in November, 1815. We had built up our Empire, and had waged no war of aggression. We were therefore content to see Holland released from her subjection to the French yoke, and to retain for ourselves, of all our captures, only Malta, Mauritius (the Ile de France), Tobago and St Lucia.

CHAPTER XIX

CONCLUSIONS

In this concluding chapter we shall make a brief survey of the naval events which succeeded the great peace of 1815, not, of course, to describe them, but to ascertain their character, and the conditions which ruled them and resulted from them, and then we may draw a general conclusion from the whole. It has been said accurately of the phrase, command of the sea, that it implies a state of war and has no special application to a state of peace. In the century which has elapsed since the great peace—a century in which our naval predominance has never been challenged—command of the sea, exercised by ourselves and our allies, has been the atmosphere in which certain things have been done.

The fighting of battles is not the common occupation of the Navy. Naval engagements are incidents of great rarity, and since Navarino the British Navy has not been concerned in one. This leads us to consider that the Navy has a function in peace as well as in war. As a modern organization it began with the activities of the old navigators, and to the names of Raleigh, Frobisher, Drake, Narborough, Dampier, Cook and Vancouver, to mention but a few, we add, in a very incomplete list, those of Ross, Franklin, Parry, Liddon, McClure, McClintock, Nares and lastly of Scott. The Navy has also taken a great part in the work of hydrography, deep-sea sounding and other branches of scientific investigation, and the *Lightning* (1868), *Porcupine* (1868–70) and *Challenger* (1872–76), were vessels which engaged in important work in this department of naval service.

In another sphere of activity the Navy, often in conditions of hardship and difficulty which are little known to the world, and often, too, in

circumstances illustrated by many brilliant fighting
episodes, has conducted a noble work for the good
of humanity in the suppression of the slave trade.
It maintained a long contest with piracy, and it
has enforced the peace and right use of the seas in
the severe repression of smuggling. On many
occasions it has protected and secured the rights of
Englishmen in foreign ports in times of civil broil
and revolution, and on not a few occasions it has
been present with its help to succour the victims of
earthquakes and distress.

The very first work of the Navy after the peace
of 1815 was, in the following year, to operate against
the pirate and slave-owning nation which was ruled
by the Dey of Algiers, and Lord Exmouth—who,
as Sir Edward Pellew, had so greatly distinguished
himself in the war—commanded an expedition which
had the effect of liberating slaves and abolishing
slavery. He enforced the *Pax Britannica*, which
replaced the anarchy of the sea. In the East, in
the Burmese wars, the Navy was largely instrumental
in laying the foundations of our rule in Burma.

When the tide in the great struggle of the Greeks
for independence had turned against them, Great
Britain was one of the powers which determined to
intervene, and in the Battle of Navarino, on the 20th
of October, 1827, the Turkish and Egyptian fleet was
destroyed, and thereby the freedom of Greece

assured. But when the ambition of Mehemet Ali threatened the integrity of Turkey, Great Britain headed a coalition against him. France took no action, but was opposed to us, and war threatened at a time when the Navy had been neglected, when comparatively few ships were in commission and the rest in a bad state, when the personnel had been reduced, and our influence rested probably more upon prestige than upon the actual possession of power.

Never, however, was there a more complete instance of the possession of sea power in an absolute form than in the Russian War of 1854–5. The world had never seen the like. The Russian fleet was completely neutralized, and the transport of troops through the Mediterranean and into the Black Sea, even including the disembarkation in the Crimea, was conducted almost as if it had been a peace operation. We did not even attempt to cover the landing of the troops by masking the Russian fleet at Sevastopol. Russia was not accessible except by sea, and the success of the whole of the operations depended upon the possession of sea power. It was the " atmosphere " in which they were conducted, but it was as little recognized by many people at the time (and since) as the atmosphere they breathed. The responsibility for the safe arrival of the troops was, of course, felt, but the worthlessness of the Russian fleet was suspected, and so little were the principles of naval warfare remembered, that the transports were apparently thought capable of protecting themselves. But if the Russians had had an effective fleet no soldier could ever have set foot in the Crimea, or, having landed, would ever have left it by sea. Yet, from the fact that the results of the war were visibly attained by military forces, it has been assumed that the Navy contributed nothing to the result.

The operations in the Baltic have attracted less notice than those in the Black Sea, but they also were of great importance, and had the effect of immobilizing large bodies of troops in Northern Russia which might otherwise have been sent to the seat of military activity. There can also be no doubt that the presence of the allied fleets in the Black Sea, and the uncertainty felt as to the places where troops might be landed, made it impossible for the Russians to locate their forces in sufficient numbers in the regions where the events proved they were actually required. Here we notice a signal mark of the effect of sea power, when, by the menace of its readiness to convey troops to one or several of many places on the enemy's coast, it paralyzes the enemy's action.

An immunity from interference or resistance at sea, similar to that which existed in the Russian War, was found in the operations for the suppression of the Indian Mutiny, and in our wars in China, South

Africa and New Zealand.   In the South African War
of 1899–1902, sea power was again the condition
which was essential for success.   Without command
of the sea, South Africa would have been lost to the
Empire.   In those years the Navy was thoroughly
efficient for all its duties, and, by patrol and control,
the transport of troops, horses and war material was
conducted with the utmost smoothness and without
any interference.   As in the Peninsular War, the
Navy gave mobility to the Army, established and
supplied its bases, and it was ready with officers, men
and guns to take part in the fighting ashore.

We have seen in the course of this inquiry,
deeply graven in the pages of history, that the Navy
has ever protected the Mother Country from invasion,
and that it has also been the creator and bond of the
Empire, the means by which the Empire has grown
and must be maintained.   It was at sea that we
vanquished the Armada, and at sea that we broke
the monopolies of Spain.   Sea power gave us
victory in our long struggle with the Dutch, and
laid the foundations of a larger dominion.   This
is the power which gave us the colonies which have
grown into the Empire, and against sea power the
ambition of Napoleon was broken and failed.

   The immunity of the kingdom from attack by
virtue of sea sea barrier properly held, has established

a settled axiom of our policy. We know it in the pages of Shakespeare. Earlier still we find it in the poem entitled "The Libel (i.e. little book) of English Policy[1]" (*circa* 1436) in the following remarkable lines :

> "Keep then the sea about in special
> Which of England is the town-wall.
> As though England were likened to a city,
> And the wall environ were the sea.
> Keep then the sea that is the wall of England;
> And then is England kept by God's hand;
> That is, for anything that is without,
> England were at ease withouten doubt."

The fact that the Empire is based on sea supremacy arises from the physical condition that the sea is all one. Wherever ships can freely go, the Empire is secure. But the protection of distant possessions, as we have seen during the long war with France, may be assured by blows struck or fleets blockaded nearer home. A fleet defeated in home waters may mean the safety of Canada, South Africa or India. A blow struck in the South Pacific may be the salvation of Australia or New Zealand. For sea communications are like streams, capable of being controlled or diverted either near their sources or at other points in their course. The strategic keys of the world are the Straits of Dover and Gibraltar,

---

[1] T. Wright, *Political Poems and Songs* (Rolls Series), vol. ii. p. 202.

the Suez Canal, and the Straits of Malacca. The
Panama Canal will be a key which we may use but
cannot hold. At and near these points and others,
hostile naval forces may be observed and controlled.
Unerring instinct and wise statesmanship, using the
Navy well, have caused us to seize and retain nearly
all the important strategical positions along the
communications of the world.

The great advantage possessed by this country
has been her position as a Sea Power alone. She
was never greatly concerned in the fighting on the
continent, except by her subsidies, until the time of
the Peninsular War, and in the campaign of Waterloo.
She has maintained her standing army upon a limited
basis almost wholly for the defence of her distant
possessions ; while the countries of the continent
have been turned into vast armed camps, absorbing
the interests, the lives and the wealth of their peoples.
The Spaniards, deeply involved in continental
strife, had no power to attain supremacy at sea. The
Dutch, embroiled in wars on land with a frontier
always threatened, and with a Navy which at one
time was every whit as good as our own, could not
maintain the fleets they had raised, and they faded
from the world-position they had won. The French,
having embarked on vast European enterprises, could
not withstand the wastage arising therefrom, which
reduced their strength at sea.

Thus, if it should be said that we have had more than our share of good fortune, that we have been aided by something like luck when on some occasions we have been endangered, and that, but for a chance which has turned against our adversaries, we should have been undone, we must remember that there is really something essentially different from the situation of other countries in the character of our kingdom and dominions, placing means at our disposal which rule and shape these things. It is our preoccupation on the sea which has given us our great seamen, for the Hawkes, Rodneys, Howes, St Vincents and Nelsons are the products of a great maritime nation, and not of one which is amphibious. We have won the rewards of sound judgment and sustained, though fluctuating, endeavour.

But we may notice also that the common experience of seamen has counselled us never to trust merely to what we have achieved. The lessons which we have learned have, in effect, been realized by other nations, who are forming navies and training them by the light of the doctrines we have taught. Material strength is much, because it gives us the machinery for action, but the action is taken by men, who are more than the machines they direct and control. Shovell and Nelson, and many other sea officers, have said they would not fight with inferior material strength if they could avoid it, but they have been much more anxious to secure the right stamp of officer and man.

The lesson, then, is that if we would secure the immunity from attack, which our forefathers have enjoyed, and would retain the Empire they have won, we must keep our Navy in both material and personal respects on a level commensurate with our responsibilities. For it is as true now, as when the words were embodied in the Naval Discipline Act, that " on the Navy, under the good Providence of God, our wealth, prosperity and peace depend."

BIBLIOGRAPHY

For the General Subject and the Early Period:

Sir NICHOLAS HARRIS NICOLAS. A History of the Royal
Navy from the earliest times to....(1422). 1847.

Rear-Admiral S. EARDLEY-WILMOT. Our Navy for a
Thousand Years. 4th edition. 1911.

DAVID HANNAY. A Short History of the Royal Navy,
1217–1815. Vol. I, 1898. Vol. II, 1909.

Commander C. N. ROBINSON, R.N. The British Fleet:
the growth, achievements and duties of the Navy of
the Empire. 1894.

Commander C. N. ROBINSON, R.N. The British Tar in
Fact and Fiction. 1909.

For the Tudor, Stuart, and Commonwealth Periods:

JULIAN S. CORBETT. Drake and the Tudor Navy. 1898.

—— The Successors of Drake. 1900.

THOMAS WEMYSS FULTON. The Sovereignty of the Sea.
1911.

Period up to the French Revolution:

Rear-Admiral A. T. MAHAN. The Influence of Sea Power
upon History, 1660–1783. 1890.

JULIAN S. CORBETT. England in the Mediterranean, 1603–
1713. 2 vols. 1904.

—— England in the Seven Years' War. 1907.

Period of the French Revolution and Empire, and the American War :

WILLIAM JAMES. The Naval History of Great Britain, 1793–1820. 1822–24.

Sir NICHOLAS HARRIS NICOLAS. The Dispatches and Letters of Vice-Admiral Lord Viscount Nelson. 1844–46.

Sir J. K. LAUGHTON. Letters and Dispatches of Horatio, Viscount Nelson. 1886.

Rear-Admiral A. T. MAHAN. The Influence of Sea Power on the French Revolution and Empire. 1892.

C. DE LA JONQUIÈRE. L'Expédition d'Égypte, 1798–1801. (n.d.)

JAMES R. THURSFIELD. Nelson and other Naval Studies. 1909.

HENRY NEWBOLT. The Year of Trafalgar. 1905.

JULIAN S. CORBETT. The Campaign of Trafalgar. 1910.

EDOUARD DESBRIÈRE. La Campagne Maritime de 1805— Trafalgar. 1907.

EDWARD FRASER. The Enemy at Trafalgar. 1906.

THEODORE ROOSEVELT. The Naval War of 1812. 1889.

Rear-Admiral A. T. MAHAN. Sea Power in its Relations to the War of 1812. 2 vols. 1905.

INDEX

www.ingramcontent.com/pod-product-compliance
Ingram Content Group UK Ltd.
Pitfield, Milton Keynes, MK11 3LW, UK
UKHW042144280225
455719UK00001B/87

9 781107 632714